The Ideal Muslim Woman

Dr. Lemu

TX0008789309

Content

* Iman (inward faith in Allah) 11
* The Ways of Attaining Faith in Allah 29
* She Worships God (Allah) Alone 39
* Women may attend the Jamaah 43
* Women may Attend Eid Prayers 65
* Sunnah and Nafil Prayer 69
* Perform Prayers Properly 75
* Righteous women must pay Zakat 81
* Righteous women fast and pray 83
* The benefits of marriage 87
* Choosing the right partner 99
* Sincerity and trust 101
* Understanding your husband 107
* Authority and obedience 111
* The family and the home 125
* Acceptance of good advice 137
* Money 141

* Friendship 145

* The sexual relationship 157

* A Co-wife (the other wife) 165

* The unreasonable husband 171

* You, your family, and Allah (swt) 183

Books by Ibn Kathir & Al-Qayyim

Stories of the Prophets
  ISBN 9781643543185
Seerah of Prophet Muhammad
  ISBN 9781094860213
Stories of the Koran
  ISBN 9781095900796
The Path to Guidance
  ISBN 9781643540818
Purification of the Soul (part 1)
  ISBN 9781643541389
Tafseer Ibn Kathir
  ISBN 9781512266573
Al-Fawaid: Wise Sayings
  ISBN 9781727812718
Heaven's Door (Purification V 2)
  ISBN 9781643541396

Soul's Journey after Death
ISBN 9781643541365
Koran: English Easy to Read
ISBN 9781643540924
Characteristics of Hypocrites
ISBN 9781643541358

Introduction

He who created death and life to test you as to which of you is best in deed - and He is the Exalted in Might, the Forgiving. (67:2)

$$\text{ٱلَّذِى خَلَقَ ٱلْمَوْتَ وَٱلْحَيَوٰةَ لِيَبْلُوَكُمْ أَيُّكُمْ أَحْسَنُ عَمَلًا وَهُوَ ٱلْعَزِيزُ ٱلْغَفُورُ ﴿٢﴾}$$

And they ask you (O Muhammad) about the Ruh (the Spirit); Say: The Ruh (the Spirit): it is one of the things, the knowledge of which is only with my Lord. And of the knowledge, you (mankind) have been given only a little. (17:85)

$$\text{وَيَسْـَٔلُونَكَ عَنِ ٱلرُّوحِ قُلِ ٱلرُّوحُ مِنْ أَمْرِ رَبِّى وَمَآ أُوتِيتُم مِّنَ ٱلْعِلْمِ إِلَّا قَلِيلًا ﴿٨٥﴾}$$

O People of the Scripture, do not commit excess in your religion or say about Allah except the truth. The Messiah, Jesus, the son of Mary, was but a messenger of Allah and His word which He directed to Mary and a soul [created at a command] from Him. So believe in Allah and His prophets and messengers. And do not say, Three; desist-it is better for you. Indeed, Allah is but one God. Exalted is He above having a son. To Allah belongs whatever is in the heavens and whatever is on the earth. And sufficient is Allah as Disposer of affairs.

يَٰٓأَهْلَ ٱلْكِتَٰبِ لَا تَغْلُوا۟ فِى دِينِكُمْ وَلَا تَقُولُوا۟ عَلَى ٱللَّهِ إِلَّا ٱلْحَقَّ إِنَّمَا ٱلْمَسِيحُ عِيسَى ٱبْنُ مَرْيَمَ رَسُولُ ٱللَّهِ وَكَلِمَتُهُۥٓ أَلْقَىٰهَآ إِلَىٰ مَرْيَمَ وَرُوحٌ مِّنْهُ فَـَٔامِنُوا۟ بِٱللَّهِ وَرُسُلِهِۦ وَلَا تَقُولُوا۟ ثَلَٰثَةٌ ٱنتَهُوا۟ خَيْرًا لَّكُمْ إِنَّمَا ٱللَّهُ إِلَٰهٌ وَٰحِدٌ سُبْحَٰنَهُۥٓ أَن يَكُونَ لَهُۥ وَلَدٌ لَّهُۥ مَا فِى ٱلسَّمَٰوَٰتِ وَمَا فِى ٱلْأَرْضِ وَكَفَىٰ بِٱللَّهِ وَكِيلًا ﴿١٧١﴾

Those Messengers! We preferred some to others; to some of them Allah spoke (directly); others He raised to degrees (of honor); and to Isa (Jesus), the son of Maryam (Mary), We gave clear proofs and evidences, and supported him with Ruh-ul-Qudus [Jibrael (Gabriel)]. If Allah had willed, succeeding generations would not have fought against each other, after clear Verses of Allah had come to them, but they differed-some of them believed and others disbelieved. If Allah had willed, they would not have fought against one another, but Allah does what He likes

﴿ تِلْكَ ٱلرُّسُلُ فَضَّلْنَا بَعْضَهُمْ عَلَىٰ بَعْضٍ مِّنْهُم مَّن كَلَّمَ ٱللَّهُ وَرَفَعَ بَعْضَهُمْ دَرَجَٰتٍ وَءَاتَيْنَا عِيسَى ٱبْنَ مَرْيَمَ ٱلْبَيِّنَٰتِ وَأَيَّدْنَٰهُ بِرُوحِ ٱلْقُدُسِ وَلَوْ شَآءَ ٱللَّهُ مَا ٱقْتَتَلَ ٱلَّذِينَ مِنۢ بَعْدِهِم مِّنۢ بَعْدِ مَا جَآءَتْهُمُ ٱلْبَيِّنَٰتُ وَلَٰكِنِ ٱخْتَلَفُوا۟ فَمِنْهُم مَّنْ ءَامَنَ وَمِنْهُم مَّن كَفَرَ وَلَوْ شَآءَ ٱللَّهُ مَا ٱقْتَتَلُوا۟ وَلَٰكِنَّ ٱللَّهَ يَفْعَلُ مَا يُرِيدُ ۝٢٥٣

Iman (inward faith in Allah)

One of the most important attributes of a good woman, is her deep faith in Allah (God), and her sincere conviction that whatever happens in this earthly life, and whatever fate befalls her, only happens through the will and decree of Allah; whatever befalls her would have been impossible to avoid, and whatever does not happen cannot be made to happen without Allah's permission.

Whoever works righteousness, man or woman, and has Faith, verily, to him will We give a new Life, a life that is good and pure and We will bestow on such their reward according to the best of their actions. (16:97)

مَنْ عَمِلَ صَٰلِحًا مِّن ذَكَرٍ أَوْ أُنثَىٰ وَهُوَ مُؤْمِنٌ فَلَنُحْيِيَنَّهُۥ حَيَوٰةً طَيِّبَةً ۖ وَلَنَجْزِيَنَّهُمْ أَجْرَهُم بِأَحْسَنِ مَا كَانُوا۟ يَعْمَلُونَ ۝٩٧

Allah hath promised the Hypocrites men and women, and the rejecters, of Faith, the fire of Hell: Therein shall they dwell: Sufficient is it for them: for them is the curse of Allah, and an enduring punishment. (9:68)

وَعَدَ ٱللَّهُ ٱلْمُنَٰفِقِينَ وَٱلْمُنَٰفِقَٰتِ وَٱلْكُفَّارَ نَارَ جَهَنَّمَ خَٰلِدِينَ فِيهَا ۚ هِىَ حَسْبُهُمْ ۚ وَلَعَنَهُمُ ٱللَّهُ ۖ وَلَهُمْ عَذَابٌ مُّقِيمٌ ۝٦٨

Humans have no choice in this life but to strive towards the Righteous Path and to do good deeds. Like acts of prayer and worship, by whatever means one can, putting all our trust in God, submitting to His will, and believing that we always in need God's help and support.

Contrary to what some believe, Allah does not prohibit women from going out to fulfill their needs. However, God lays down a proper code of behavior, which is primarily intended to safeguard the modesty, dignity and honor of men and women.

On that day you will see the faithful men and the faithful women -- their light running before them and on their right hand-- good news for you today: gardens beneath which rivers flow, to abide therein, that is the grand achievement. (57:12)

يَوْمَ تَرَى ٱلْمُؤْمِنِينَ وَٱلْمُؤْمِنَٰتِ يَسْعَىٰ نُورُهُم بَيْنَ أَيْدِيهِمْ وَبِأَيْمَٰنِهِم بُشْرَىٰكُمُ ٱلْيَوْمَ جَنَّٰتٌ تَجْرِى مِن تَحْتِهَا ٱلْأَنْهَٰرُ خَٰلِدِينَ فِيهَا ۚ ذَٰلِكَ هُوَ ٱلْفَوْزُ ٱلْعَظِيمُ ۝١٢

"O my Lord! Forgive me, my parents, all who enter my house in Faith, and (all) believing men and believing women: and to the wrong-doers grant Thou no increase but in perdition! (71:28)

رَّبِّ ٱغْفِرْ لِى وَلِوَٰلِدَىَّ وَلِمَن دَخَلَ بَيْتِىَ مُؤْمِنًا وَلِلْمُؤْمِنِينَ وَٱلْمُؤْمِنَٰتِ وَلَا تَزِدِ ٱلظَّٰلِمِينَ إِلَّا تَبَارًۢا ۝٢٨

Allah, the Creator of humans, knows our nature better than anyone, and thus God has prescribed appropriate rules of behavior and appearance to be observed when men and women interact with one another in a social milieu. These rules of interaction also include a prescription for modesty in dress, talk and walk, etc.

1- Lowering the gaze: Indeed it is the most precious ornament of a woman is modesty, and the best expression of modesty is in the lowering of the gaze, as Almighty Allah says, [...And tell the believing women that they should lower their gazes...] (An-Nur 24: 31)

2- Not intermingling with any men in such a way that their bodies come in contact or that a man touches women, as happens so often happens at the market.

It is better for one of you to be pricked in the head with an iron pick than to touch a woman whom it is unlawful to touch.

Tell the believing men to lower their gaze (from looking at forbidden things), and protect their private parts (from illegal sexual acts, etc.). That is purer for them. Verily, Allah is All-Aware of what they do. (24:30)

قُل لِّلْمُؤْمِنِينَ يَغُضُّوا مِنْ أَبْصَٰرِهِمْ وَيَحْفَظُوا فُرُوجَهُمْ ذَٰلِكَ أَزْكَىٰ لَهُمْ إِنَّ ٱللَّهَ خَبِيرٌۢ بِمَا يَصْنَعُونَ ۝

3- Her clothing must conform to the standards laid down by God:

a) Her dress must cover her entire body with the exception of [that which is apparent] (An-Nur 24: 31) which, refers to the face and hands.

b) It must never be transparent, revealing what is underneath it. The Prophet (peace and blessings be upon him) has informed us that, "Among the dwellers of hell are such women as are clothed yet naked, seducing and being seduced.

These shall not enter the Beautiful Garden, nor shall (even) its fragrance reach them. "Here, the meaning of "clothed yet naked" is that their light, thin, transparent garments do not conceal what is underneath.

c) Her dress must not be too tight so as to define the parts of her beautiful body, especially its curves, even though it may not be transparent. This describes many of the styles of clothing current our current world.

Women who wear such clothes likewise fall under the definition of "clothed but naked", since such a dress is often more provocative than one which is transparent.

d) She should never wear clothes which are specifically for men, such as trousers.

God's Prophet (peace and blessings be upon him) was very sad when he saw women trying to resemble men and men trying to resemble women.

He prohibited women from wearing men's clothing and vice-versa.

e) In her choice of clothing, a woman should try not to imitate others, for Islam disapproves of conformity to non-Islamic modes and desires its men and women to develop their own distinctive characteristics in appearance, as well as in beliefs and excellent attitudes.

God's Prophet (peace and blessings be upon him) said:

"Whoever imitates a people is one of them."

And as for women past child-bearing who do not expect wed-lock, it is no sin on them if they discard their (outer) clothing in such a way as not to show their adornment.

But to refrain (i.e. not to discard their outer clothing) is better for them. And Allah is All-Hearer, All-Knower. (24:60)

وَٱلْقَوَٰعِدُ مِنَ ٱلنِّسَآءِ ٱلَّٰتِى لَا يَرْجُونَ نِكَاحًا فَلَيْسَ عَلَيْهِنَّ جُنَاحٌ أَن يَضَعْنَ ثِيَابَهُنَّ غَيْرَ مُتَبَرِّجَٰتٍۭ بِزِينَةٍ ۖ وَأَن يَسْتَعْفِفْنَ خَيْرٌ لَّهُنَّ ۗ وَٱللَّهُ سَمِيعٌ عَلِيمٌ ۝

4- A woman that loves Allah must walk and talk in a dignified and business-like manner, avoiding flirtatiousness in her facial expressions and movements. Please remember that flirting and seductive behavior are characteristics of wrong-minded women, not of Muslims.

Allah said: [Then do not be too pleasant of speech, lest one in whose heart there is a disease should feel desire (for you) …] (Al-Ahzab 33:32)

يَٰنِسَآءَ ٱلنَّبِيِّ لَسۡتُنَّ كَأَحَدٖ مِّنَ ٱلنِّسَآءِۚ إِنِ ٱتَّقَيۡتُنَّ فَلَا تَخۡضَعۡنَ بِٱلۡقَوۡلِ فَيَطۡمَعَ ٱلَّذِي فِي قَلۡبِهِۦ مَرَضٞ وَقُلۡنَ قَوۡلٗا مَّعۡرُوفٗا ﴿٣٢﴾

And tell the believing women to lower their gaze (from looking at forbidden things), and protect their private parts (from illegal sexual acts, etc.) and not to show off their adornment except only that which is apparent (like palms of hands or one eye or both eyes for necessity to see the way, or outer dress like veil, gloves, head-cover, apron, etc.), and to draw their veils all over Juyubihinna (i.e. their bodies, faces, necks and bosoms, etc.) and not to reveal their adornment except to their husbands, their fathers, their husband's fathers, their sons, their husband's sons, their brothers or their brother's sons, or their sister's sons, or their (Muslim) women (i.e. their sisters in Islam), or the (female) slaves whom their right hands possess, or old male servants who lack vigor, or small children who have no sense of the shame of sex. And let them not stamp their feet so as to reveal what they hide of their adornment. And all of you beg Allah to forgive you all, O believers, that you may be successful.

وَقُل لِّلْمُؤْمِنَٰتِ يَغْضُضْنَ مِنْ أَبْصَٰرِهِنَّ وَيَحْفَظْنَ فُرُوجَهُنَّ وَلَا يُبْدِينَ زِينَتَهُنَّ إِلَّا مَا ظَهَرَ مِنْهَا وَلْيَضْرِبْنَ بِخُمُرِهِنَّ عَلَىٰ جُيُوبِهِنَّ وَلَا يُبْدِينَ زِينَتَهُنَّ إِلَّا لِبُعُولَتِهِنَّ أَوْ ءَابَآئِهِنَّ أَوْ ءَابَآءِ بُعُولَتِهِنَّ أَوْ أَبْنَآئِهِنَّ أَوْ أَبْنَآءِ بُعُولَتِهِنَّ أَوْ إِخْوَٰنِهِنَّ أَوْ بَنِىٓ إِخْوَٰنِهِنَّ أَوْ بَنِىٓ أَخَوَٰتِهِنَّ أَوْ نِسَآئِهِنَّ أَوْ مَا مَلَكَتْ أَيْمَٰنُهُنَّ أَوِ ٱلتَّٰبِعِينَ غَيْرِ أُو۟لِى ٱلْإِرْبَةِ مِنَ ٱلرِّجَالِ أَوِ ٱلطِّفْلِ ٱلَّذِينَ لَمْ يَظْهَرُوا۟ عَلَىٰ عَوْرَٰتِ ٱلنِّسَآءِ وَلَا يَضْرِبْنَ بِأَرْجُلِهِنَّ لِيُعْلَمَ مَا يُخْفِينَ مِن زِينَتِهِنَّ وَتُوبُوٓا۟ إِلَى ٱللَّهِ جَمِيعًا أَيُّهَ ٱلْمُؤْمِنُونَ لَعَلَّكُمْ تُفْلِحُونَ ﴿٣١﴾

5- A woman that loves Allah does not draw men's attention to her concealed adornment by the use of perfume or by jingling or toying with her ornaments or other such things. Many such women in the time of jahiliyyah (before the Prophet was sent) used to stamp their feet like donkeys when they passed by men so that the jingling of their ankle-bracelets might be heard.

Allah forbade this, both because it might tempt a weak man to pursue her and also because it demonstrates the evil intention of the woman in attempting to draw the attention of men to herself. Allah said: [They should not strike their feet in order to make known what they hide of their adornment...] (An-Nur 24:31)

O Prophet! When believing women come to you to give you the Bai'a (pledge), that they will not associate anything in worship with Allah, that they will not steal, that they will not commit illegal sexual intercourse, that they will not kill their children, that they will not utter slander, intentionally forging falsehood (i.e. by making illegal children belonging to their husbands), and that they will not disobey you in any Ma'ruf (Islamic Monotheism and all that which Islam ordains) then accept their Bai'a (pledge), and ask Allah to forgive them, Verily, Allah is Oft-Forgiving, Most Merciful.

يَٰٓأَيُّهَا ٱلنَّبِيُّ إِذَا جَآءَكَ ٱلْمُؤْمِنَٰتُ يُبَايِعْنَكَ عَلَىٰٓ أَن لَّا يُشْرِكْنَ بِٱللَّهِ شَيْـًٔا وَلَا يَسْرِقْنَ وَلَا يَزْنِينَ وَلَا يَقْتُلْنَ أَوْلَٰدَهُنَّ وَلَا يَأْتِينَ بِبُهْتَٰنٍ يَفْتَرِينَهُۥ بَيْنَ أَيْدِيهِنَّ وَأَرْجُلِهِنَّ وَلَا يَعْصِينَكَ فِى مَعْرُوفٍ ۙ فَبَايِعْهُنَّ وَٱسْتَغْفِرْ لَهُنَّ ٱللَّهَ ۖ إِنَّ ٱللَّهَ غَفُورٌ رَّحِيمٌ ﴿١٢﴾

The Prophet's (peace be upon him) said: "The woman who perfumes herself and passes through a gathering is an adulteress."

"Any woman who perfumes herself and passes by a group of people so that her scent reaches them is an adulteress."

Allah does not require, as many people claim, that a woman must remain confined to her house until death takes her out to her grave. On the contrary, a woman may go out for prayer, for her studies, and for her other lawful needs, both religious and secular, as was customary among the women of the families of the Companions and the women of later generations.

Moreover, this early period, during the Prophet's time, we consider to be the best and most exemplary period in history. Among the women of this time were those who took part in battles in the company of the Prophet himself (peace and blessings be upon him), and after that under the caliphs (rulers) and their commanders. The Messenger of Allah (peace and blessings be upon him) told his wife Sawdah, "God has permitted you to go out for your needs. "He also said, "If someone's wife asks his permission to go to God's House (Masjid), he should not deny it to her."

Indeed Allah has heard the statement of her (Khaulah bint Tha'labah) that disputes with you (O Muhammad SAW) concerning her husband (Aus bin As-Samit), and complains to Allah. And Allah hears the argument between you both. Verily, Allah is All-Hearer, All-Seer. (58:1)

قَدْ سَمِعَ ٱللَّهُ قَوْلَ ٱلَّتِي تُجَٰدِلُكَ فِي زَوْجِهَا وَتَشْتَكِىٓ إِلَى ٱللَّهِ وَٱللَّهُ يَسْمَعُ تَحَاوُرَكُمَآ إِنَّ ٱللَّهَ سَمِيعٌۢ بَصِيرٌ ﴿١﴾

The Ways of Attaining Faith in Allah

When any person looks at anything, he notices every particle in this life requires a cause for its existence, it either gives existence to itself or something gives it existence. But if it is not possible for it to give existence to itself, how could it give existence to anything else? Look at a tree, from its stem to the leaves; indeed, it is a marvellous beauty that amazes the intellects. What gave each one of the cells of the leaves the power to absorb water and nourishment from the depths of the earth? "He causes it to grow for you. Indeed in it is a sign for a people who give thought." (16:11)

يُنۢبِتُ لَكُم بِهِ ٱلزَّرْعَ وَٱلزَّيْتُونَ وَٱلنَّخِيلَ وَٱلْأَعْنَٰبَ وَمِن كُلِّ ٱلثَّمَرَٰتِۗ إِنَّ فِى ذَٰلِكَ لَءَايَةً لِّقَوْمٍ يَتَفَكَّرُونَ ﴿١١﴾

"And who believe in what has been revealed to you, [O Muhammad], and what was revealed before you, and of the Hereafter they are certain [in faith]." (2:4)

وَٱلَّذِينَ يُؤْمِنُونَ بِمَا أُنزِلَ إِلَيْكَ وَمَا أُنزِلَ مِن قَبْلِكَ وَبِٱلْأَخِرَةِ هُمْ يُوقِنُونَ ﴿٤﴾

We have no choice in this life but to do good deeds, like acts of worship and prayer. One must always put all their trust in God and submitting to His will always. If Allah helps you, none can overcome you; and if He forsakes you, who is there after Him that can help you? And in Allah (Alone) let believers put their trust. (3:160)

إِن يَنصُرْكُمُ ٱللَّهُ فَلَا غَالِبَ لَكُمْ ۖ وَإِن يَخْذُلْكُمْ فَمَن ذَا ٱلَّذِى يَنصُرُكُم مِّنۢ بَعْدِهِۦ ۗ وَعَلَى ٱللَّهِ فَلْيَتَوَكَّلِ ٱلْمُؤْمِنُونَ ﴿١٦٠﴾

The story of Hajar gives all of us the most beautiful example of the deep faith in God (Allah) and sincere trust in Him. Prophet Ibrahim, May peace be upon him always, left his wife at the House of Allah in Makkah, above the well of Zamzam. At that time there were no people and no water there at all. Hajar had no-one with her except her baby son, Ismail. She asked her husband Ibrahim, calmly and kindly: "Has God commanded you to leave us here?" Ibrahim replied, "Yes!" Her response showed her acceptance and optimism: "Then God is not going to abandon us."

"O our Lord! I have made some of my offspring to dwell in an uncultivable valley by Your Sacred House (the Ka'bah at Makkah); in order, O our Lord, that they may perform As-Salat (Iqamat-as-Salat), so fill some hearts among men with love towards them, and (O Allah) provide them with fruits so that they may give thanks. (14:37)

رَّبَّنَآ إِنِّىٓ أَسْكَنتُ مِن ذُرِّيَّتِى بِوَادٍ غَيْرِ ذِى زَرْعٍ عِندَ بَيْتِكَ ٱلْمُحَرَّمِ رَبَّنَا لِيُقِيمُوا۟ ٱلصَّلَوٰةَ فَٱجْعَلْ أَفْـِٔدَةً مِّنَ ٱلنَّاسِ تَهْوِىٓ إِلَيْهِمْ وَٱرْزُقْهُم مِّنَ ٱلثَّمَرَٰتِ لَعَلَّهُمْ يَشْكُرُونَ ﴿٣٧﴾

Here was a truly difficult situation: a man leaving his wife and baby son in a barren, hot, and dry land, where there were no plants, not even water, animals, or anyone.

Ibrahim was told to go back to the distant land of Palestine without his wife and son. He left nothing with Hajar but a small sack of dates (fruit) and a skin filled with very little water. Were it not for her deep faith and trust in God that filled her heart, Hajar would not have been able to cope with such a sad situation.

She would have fainted straight away, and would not have become the strong woman whose name is forever remembered. For example, each time a Muslim performs hajj or umrah at the House of God, they drink the pure water of Zamzam, and run between the mounts of Safa and Marwah remembering Hajar, as Hajar done on that most difficult day. Through the many centuries, Hajar's deep faith and her love of God had an amazing effect on the lives of men and women. Hajar awoke their consciences and reminded them that God knows every secret, and that He is with you wherever you may be. It is impossible to hide from God.

Narrated Abdullah ibn Zayd ibn Aslam, his grandfather said: `One day when I was accompanying Omar on his patrol at night, Omar felt tired, so he put his back against some wall.

It was a dark without a moon, then we heard a woman saying to her daughter, "My daughter, stand-up and mix the milk with some water." Then her daughter said, "Mother, you did not hear the decree of Omar (chief of the believers) today?" The mother said, "What Omar said?" The daughter said, "He ordered his assistant to announce that milk must never be mixed with water." The mother said, "Just mix the milk with water; you are in my house, Omar cannot see you." Her daughter replied, "But God sees everything." `Omar heard this, and said "Go to that house and see who is that girl and whether she has a husband?"

So I went to that house, and I learned that she was not married. The other woman was her mother. I came to Omar and told him the story.

He called his sons, and said to them: "Do any of you need a good wife? If I was younger and I had the desire to get married, I would marry this beautiful hearted woman." Abdullah said: "I have a good wife." Abd al-Rahman said: "I also have a good wife." Asim said: "Father, I do not have a wife, so please let me marry her." So Omar arranged for her to be married to his son Asim. She gave him a daughter, who grew up to be the mother of Omar ibn Abd al-Aziz.'" Omar al-Aziz became a caliph and ruled from 717 to 720. This young woman was righteous and honest in all her deeds, both in public and in private, because she believed that God was with her at all times and God sees and hears everything. This is true faith (Emman). One of the immediate rewards that God gave her was this blessed marriage.

A true and pure faith increases the character and weight of a woman in maturity, strength, and understanding, so she sees earthly life clearly.

Life is just a place of worship and testing. The results will be seen on the Day of Judgment. On that Day, all of mankind will be brought in front of God to account for their deeds. If their deeds are good, it will be good for them. God is fair in His judgment. There will not be the slightest injustice: On that Day, every soul will be rewarded for what it earned. No injustice will there be on that Day. (40:17)

ٱلۡيَوۡمَ تُجۡزَىٰ كُلُّ نَفۡسٍ بِمَا كَسَبَتۡ لَا ظُلۡمَ ٱلۡيَوۡمَ إِنَّ ٱللَّهَ سَرِيعُ ٱلۡحِسَابِ ۝

On that Day, every deed will be measured to the utmost precision. If anyone did an atom's weight of good, then they shall see it! And if anyone did an atom's weight of evil, they shall see it. (99:7-8)

فَمَن يَعۡمَلۡ مِثۡقَالَ ذَرَّةٍ خَيۡرًا يَرَهُۥ ۝

وَمَن يَعْمَلْ مِثْقَالَ ذَرَّةٍ شَرًّا يَرَهُۥ ۝

And We shall set up balances of justice on the Day of Resurrection, then none will be dealt with unjustly in anything. And if there be the weight of a mustard seed, We will bring it. And Sufficient are We as Reckoners. (21:47)

وَنَضَعُ ٱلْمَوَٰزِينَ ٱلْقِسْطَ لِيَوْمِ ٱلْقِيَٰمَةِ فَلَا تُظْلَمُ نَفْسٌ شَيْـًٔا ۖ وَإِن كَانَ مِثْقَالَ حَبَّةٍ مِّنْ خَرْدَلٍ أَتَيْنَا بِهَا ۗ وَكَفَىٰ بِنَا حَٰسِبِينَ ۝

She Worships God (Allah) Alone

A good woman worships her Lord each day. She worship no other besides Him. She knows that she must observe and obey all of His commandments. She offers each of the prayers on time. She does not invent excuses, and never let her chores prevent her from praying on time. Worship and prayer are the pillar of religion, and whoever neglects prayer destroys the faith. Prayer is the most noble of deeds. The Prophet, Peace and Blessing be upon him, was asked: `What deed is most loved by God (Allah)?' The Prophet replied: `To offer each prayer on time, and to treat your own parents with lots of respect and mercy.' Prayer is the rope that pulls God and man together. It is the link between the servant and the Lord. It is like a well from which a person quenches their nourishment and gets strength and contentment, and it cleanses the stains of sin.

The Messenger of Allah (peace and blessings be upon him) said: "What would you say if there was a beautiful river running by your door, and you bathed in it at least 5 times a day, would any dirt be left on you?" The people said: "No!" The Prophet said: "This is exactly like the 5 daily prayers, through which Allah erases sins."

And seek help through patience and prayer, and indeed, it is difficult except for the humbly submissive [to Allah] (2:45)

وَٱسْتَعِينُوا۟ بِٱلصَّبْرِ وَٱلصَّلَوٰةِ وَإِنَّهَا لَكَبِيرَةٌ إِلَّا عَلَى ٱلْخَٰشِعِينَ

Prayer is a mercy, which God has bestowed upon His creation. We seek its shade 5 times a day and praise God, glorifying Him, and asking for His help, mercy, guidance, and forgiveness.

So prayer is a means of purification for those who pray. Prayer washes our sins away.

And establish prayer and give zakah, and whatever good you put forward for yourselves - you will find it with Allah. Indeed, Allah of what you do, is Seeing. (2:110)

وَأَقِيمُوا۟ ٱلصَّلَوٰةَ وَءَاتُوا۟ ٱلزَّكَوٰةَ وَمَا تُقَدِّمُوا۟ لِأَنفُسِكُم مِّنْ خَيْرٍ تَجِدُوهُ عِندَ ٱللَّهِ إِنَّ ٱللَّهَ بِمَا تَعْمَلُونَ بَصِيرٌ ۝

The Prophet (peace and blessings be upon him) said: "When the time for prayer comes, if you do good wudu (wash) properly, then you concentrate on the prayer and bow correctly, your prayer will then be an expiation for the sins committed prior to it, as long as you committed no major sins. This is the case until the end." (Sahih Muslim 3/112).

Women may attend the Jamaah (Congregational) Prayer in the Masjid (Mosque)

Allah has exempted all women from the obligation to attend Friday and the jamaah prayer in the masjid. However, women may attend jamaah prayer if they want to, but must dress well so not to cause temptations. And indeed, the first women in Islam did pray in the masjid behind the Prophet (peace and blessings be upon him).

Aisha (May Allah be pleased with her) (the wife of the Prophet) said: "The Messenger of Allah (peace and blessings be upon him) used to pray Fajr (Morning Prayer), and the believing women prayed behind him. They were wrapped up in their outer garments, and afterwards they went back to their homes, and no Muslim man bothered them."

O Prophet! Tell your wives and your daughters and the women of the believers to draw their cloaks (veils) all over their bodies. That will be better, that they should be known (as free respectable women) so as not to be annoyed. And Allah is Ever OftForgiving, Most Merciful. (33:59)

يَٰٓأَيُّهَا ٱلنَّبِىُّ قُل لِّأَزْوَٰجِكَ وَبَنَاتِكَ وَنِسَآءِ ٱلْمُؤْمِنِينَ يُدْنِينَ عَلَيْهِنَّ مِن جَلَٰبِيبِهِنَّ ۚ ذَٰلِكَ أَدْنَىٰٓ أَن يُعْرَفْنَ فَلَا يُؤْذَيْنَ ۗ وَكَانَ ٱللَّهُ غَفُورًا رَّحِيمًا ۝

The Prophet (peace be upon him) always shortened the prayer if he heard a baby or child crying. The Prophet (peace and blessings be upon him) said: "I always began each prayer intending to make it lengthy, but if I heard a child crying, I shortened the prayer, because I knew the stress the mother might be feeling because of the crying."

Allah showed great mercy to all women by sparing them from offering the 5 compulsory prayers in congregation, in the masjid. If Allah had made it obligatory on women as well, then it would have placed a tough burden on many women, and they may not have been able to do it, as we can see many men failing to pray on a regular basis in the masjid.

If woman asks her husband for permission to go to the masjid, her husband is not allowed to stop her, as the Prophet said in a number of hadith: "Even though their houses are better for them, do not stop your women from going to the masjid. If the wife of any man wants to go to the masjid, do not stop her."

The men of that time, heeded the words and command of the Prophet (peace and blessings be upon him), and allowed their women to go out to the masjid, even if it was against their own wishes. There is no clearer sign of this matter than the hadith of Abdullah ibn Omar, in which he said: Omar's wife used to pray Fajr and Isha prayers in the masjid, and she was asked: "Why do you go to the masjid when you know that your husband, Omar, dislikes this and he is also a very jealous man?" She said: "What is stopping Omar from stopping me?" They said: "the words of the Messenger of Allah (peace and blessings be upon him): never stop any female servants of Allah from attending the masjid of Allah."

The Prophet allowed women to attend the masjid, and prohibited men from stopping them from doing so. The Masajid became full of women coming and going, both at the time of the Prophet (peace be upon him), and in later periods. Indeed, the Muslim men and Muslim women, the believing men and believing women, the obedient men and obedient women, the truthful men and truthful women, the patient men and patient women, the humble men and humble women, the charitable men and charitable women, the fasting men and fasting women, the men who guard their private parts and the women who do so, and the men who remember Allah often and the women who do so - for them Allah has prepared forgiveness and a great reward. (33:35)

إِنَّ ٱلْمُسْلِمِينَ وَٱلْمُسْلِمَٰتِ وَٱلْمُؤْمِنِينَ وَٱلْمُؤْمِنَٰتِ وَٱلْقَٰنِتِينَ وَٱلْقَٰنِتَٰتِ وَٱلصَّٰدِقِينَ وَٱلصَّٰدِقَٰتِ وَٱلصَّٰبِرِينَ وَٱلصَّٰبِرَٰتِ وَٱلْخَٰشِعِينَ وَٱلْخَٰشِعَٰتِ وَٱلْمُتَصَدِّقِينَ وَٱلْمُتَصَدِّقَٰتِ وَٱلصَّٰٓئِمِينَ وَٱلصَّٰٓئِمَٰتِ وَٱلْحَٰفِظِينَ فُرُوجَهُمْ وَٱلْحَٰفِظَٰتِ وَٱلذَّٰكِرِينَ ٱللَّهَ كَثِيرًا وَٱلذَّٰكِرَٰتِ أَعَدَّ ٱللَّهُ لَهُم مَّغْفِرَةً وَأَجْرًا عَظِيمًا ﴿٣٥﴾

Many women went to pray, listen to lectures, and took part in the public life of Islam. When the command from Allah came to take the Kabbah as the new qiblah (the direction to turn during prayer), the men and women who were praying and facing towards Palestine, turned to face the direction of the Kabbah.

This means that the women and men that were praying together, had to change places. The masjid is the center of light and guidance for men and women. From the dawn of Islam, women had their role to play in the masjid.

There are many sahih reports and books that confirm the woman's presence and their role in the masjid. The reports describe how women attended regular prayer, the Eid prayers, the eclipse prayer, and responding to the call of the muezzin to join the prayer.

The Prophet (peace and blessings be upon) taught everyone to present a neat and clean appearance at Friday and jumuah prayers by encouraging them to take a shower. The Prophet said: "Whoever comes to jumuah prayer, men or women, they should take a shower first." Hadith reports also tell us about Asma bint, daughter of Abu Bakr (May Allah be pleased with her). She attended the eclipse prayer (salat al-kusuf) with the Prophet (peace and blessings be upon him). Asma could not hear the Prophet's words clearly, so she asked a man who was nearby what the Prophet said.

This hadith is reported by Bukhari: "The Messenger of Allah (peace be upon him) stood up to address the people (after the eclipse prayer), and spoke about the testing that all humans will undergo in the grave. When he mentioned that, the people panicked and were loud, and so this prevented Asma from hearing the latter part of the Prophet's speech.

When the noise died down, Asma asked a man who was nearby, `May Allah bless you, what did the Messenger of Allah say?' The main said, "It was revealed to the Prophet (peace be upon him) that everyone will be tested in the grave with something similar in severity to the test (fitnah) of the Dajjal."

And verily, for those who do wrong, there is another punishment (i.e. the torment in this world and in their graves) before this, but most of them know not. (52:47)

وَإِنَّ لِلَّذِينَ ظَلَمُوا عَذَابًا دُونَ ذَٰلِكَ وَلَٰكِنَّ أَكْثَرَهُمْ لَا يَعْلَمُونَ ﴿٤٧﴾

Indeed, your Lord knows, that you stand [in prayer] almost two thirds of the night or half of it or a third of it, and [so do] a group of those with you. And Allah determines [the extent of] the night and the day.

Allah knows that you [Muslims] will not be able to do it and has turned to you in forgiveness, so recite what is easy [for you] of the Quran. He has known that there will be among you those who are ill and others traveling throughout the land seeking [something] of the bounty of Allah and others fighting for the cause of Allah. So recite what is easy from it and establish prayer and give zakah and loan Allah a goodly loan. And whatever good you put forward for yourselves - you will find it with Allah. It is better and greater in reward. And seek forgiveness of Allah. Indeed, Allah is Forgiving and Merciful. (73:20)

۞ إِنَّ رَبَّكَ يَعْلَمُ أَنَّكَ تَقُومُ أَدْنَىٰ مِن ثُلُثَيِ ٱلَّيْلِ وَنِصْفَهُۥ وَثُلُثَهُۥ وَطَآئِفَةٌ مِّنَ ٱلَّذِينَ مَعَكَۚ وَٱللَّهُ يُقَدِّرُ ٱلَّيْلَ وَٱلنَّهَارَۚ عَلِمَ أَن لَّن تُحْصُوهُ فَتَابَ عَلَيْكُمْۖ فَٱقْرَءُوا۟ مَا تَيَسَّرَ مِنَ ٱلْقُرْءَانِۚ عَلِمَ أَن سَيَكُونُ مِنكُم مَّرْضَىٰ وَءَاخَرُونَ يَضْرِبُونَ فِى ٱلْأَرْضِ يَبْتَغُونَ مِن فَضْلِ ٱللَّهِ وَءَاخَرُونَ يُقَـٰتِلُونَ فِى سَبِيلِ ٱللَّهِۖ فَٱقْرَءُوا۟ مَا تَيَسَّرَ مِنْهُۚ وَأَقِيمُوا۟ ٱلصَّلَوٰةَ وَءَاتُوا۟ ٱلزَّكَوٰةَ وَأَقْرِضُوا۟ ٱللَّهَ قَرْضًا حَسَنًاۚ وَمَا تُقَدِّمُوا۟ لِأَنفُسِكُم مِّنْ خَيْرٍ تَجِدُوهُ عِندَ ٱللَّهِ هُوَ خَيْرًا وَأَعْظَمَ أَجْرًاۚ وَٱسْتَغْفِرُوا۟ ٱللَّهَۖ إِنَّ ٱللَّهَ غَفُورٌ رَّحِيمٌۢ ﴿٢٠﴾

Muslim and Bukhari narrated another report from Asma, in which she said: "There was a solar eclipse at the time of the Prophet (peace and blessings be upon him).

I saw the Messenger of Allah (peace and blessings be upon him) standing (in prayer), so I joined him. The Prophet was standing for so long that I felt I tired, but then I noticed an old woman who was tired and weak, then I said to myself: The woman looks much weaker than I, so I must continue to stand. Then the Prophet (peace be upon him) bowed, and again remained in that position for a long time; then the Prophet (peace be upon him) raised his head and stood for a long time. So if anyone entered the Masjid at this point they might think that the Prophet had not yet bowed in ruku. The Prophet then completed the prayer when the eclipse was over. He addressed the people, praising and glorifying Allah the Almighty."

During that golden era, the time of the Prophet (peace and blessings be upon him), women knew about their own religion and were aware about the affairs that concerned the Muslims in this world and the next. When women heard the call to prayer, they rushed to the masjid to hear the Prophet (peace and blessings be upon him).

Fatimah bint Qays, one of the earliest migrant women (muhajirat), said: "The prayer was called, so I hurried with the others to the masjid, and prayed with the Messenger of Allah (peace and blessings be upon him). I was in the first row for women, which was just behind the last row of men."

Some people tend to believe that woman at the back row in prayer, behind the last row of men, means that women are lower and less deserving and men have power.

This is not correct. The reason for this is twofold: (i) Men are not disciplined often, and (ii) Women are far more disciplined.

If you think about it, when we were children in school, the disciplined students would often sit in the back of the classroom, while those children who were a bit rowdy, the teacher would sit them in the front.

Initially, at the Masjid al-Nabawi, both men and women entered the masjid through the same door. When this caused overcrowding on entrances and exits, the Messenger of Allah (peace and blessings be upon him) said: "It would be better if this door of the Masjid is left for women." Upon this, the door became known up until today as: "The Women's Door" or Bab al-Nisa.

It is very clear, from many sahih reports, that women went to the masjid on various occasions and that this attendance was an approved custom at the time of the Prophet (peace and blessings be upon him). Even when a woman was attacked once on her way to the masjid, this incident did not make the Prophet (peace and blessings be upon him) have any reservations about allowing women to go to the masjid.

The Prophet still allowed women to do what made them happy, and prohibited men preventing them, because there is so much benefit, spiritual, knowledge, mental, and otherwise, for women in attending prayers and lectures at the masjid.

Wail al-Kindi reported that a good woman was once attacked by a man in the early morning, while she was on her way to the masjid for Fajr prayer. The woman shouted to a passer-by for help, then a large group of men ran to her. Instead they seized the man to whom she had first called for help, so her attacker ran away. They brought the innocent man to her, and he said: "But I am the one who answered your call for help; your attacker got away."

They brought the man to the Messenger of Allah (peace and blessings be upon him), and told him that this man had attacked the woman. However, the man said: "I was the one who answered her call for help against her attacker, but these people seized me and brought me here." The woman said: "He is lying; he is the one who attacked me."

The Messenger of Allah (peace be upon him) said: "Take him away and stone him." But then another man stood up and said, "Please do not stone him, stone me instead, for I am the one who attacked the woman." Now the Messenger of Allah (peace and blessings be upon him) had three people before him: the man who had attacked the woman, the man who had answered her calls for help, and the woman.

The Prophet (peace and blessings be upon him) told the attacker: "As for you, Allah has forgiven you for your honesty," and the Prophet spoke kind words to the one who had helped the woman. Then Omar said: "Stone the one who has admitted to the crime of adultery." But the Prophet (peace be upon him) said: "No, for he has repented to Allah by speaking the truth, saving this man's life, and asking to be stoned instead.

His act of repentance and truthfulness was so great that if the people were to repent in this manner always, it would be accepted from them."

The Messenger of Allah (peace and blessings be upon him) appreciated the circumstances of the women that attended the congregational prayers, so he was kind to the women, and he would always shorten the prayer if he heard a child crying, so that the mother would never become distressed and tired. Many sahih reports describe how the Prophet (peace and blessings be upon him) used to organize women at congregational prayers, for example: "The best row for men is the front, and the worst is the back row; the best row for women is at the back, and the worst row is at the front." Another hadith report, deals with allowing women to leave the masjid before the men, after the prayer is over.

Hind bint al-Harith said that Umm Salamah, the wife of the Prophet (peace and blessings be upon him), told her that when the obligatory prayer was over, women before the men would get up to leave.

The Messenger of Allah (peace and blessings be upon him) and the men would wait as long as Allah willed. When the Prophet (peace and blessings be upon him) got up to leave, the men would only then get up to leave.

Muslim and Bukhari also reported a hadith concerning how a woman can draw the imam's attention to something during the prayer by clapping. Sahl ibn Sa'd al-Sa'idi said: "The Messenger of Allah (peace and blessings be upon him) said: 'Why do I see you clapping so much?

Whoever notices any error in my prayer should say 'Subhan Allah,' for by doing so he will alert me to the error. Clapping is only for women.'" The number of women that attended the masjid increased daily until, at the time of the Abbasids, the women filled the courtyard of the masjid, and men would have no choice but to pray behind them.

This was the verdict (fatwa) of Imam Malik, Ibn al-Qasim said: "I asked Imam Malik about the men who come to the masjid and found the courtyard filled with women, and the masjid itself filled with men. May those men pray behind the women?" Malik said: 'Yes their prayer is valid.'" However, women going out to the masjid must be careful not a cause fitnah (temptations). Men and women must always behave in accordance with the Prophet's teachings of purity of thought and behavior.

If for any reason there is the fear of temptations, then it is best for women to pray at home. This is what is indicated by the hadith of the Prophet (peace and blessings be upon him): "Do not stop your women from going to the masjid, although their houses are better for them."

However, some men feared the possibility of fitnah, and so they took this as an excuse to prohibit their women from going to the masjid. So the Prophet (peace and blessings be upon him) said: "Do not prevent the women from going to the masjid at night." One of the sons of Abdullah ibn Omar said: "We will not let women go out because it will give rise to deviation and suspicion." Ibn Omar scolded him and said: "I tell you that the Messenger of Allah (peace be upon him) said such-and-such and you say: 'No, we will not let them!'"

It is also permissible for women to attend the gatherings of the Muslims in the masjid. There is a lot to be gained from this. However, certain conditions apply to this permission. The most important of which is that women who go to the masjid must not wear perfume or make-up. Zaynab al-Thaqafiyyah said that the Prophet (peace and blessings be upon him) said: "If any woman want to attend Isha prayer, they she should not wear perfume."

O Prophet, say to your wives, "If you should desire the worldly life and its adornment, then come, I will provide for you and give you a gracious release. (33:28)

يَٰٓأَيُّهَا ٱلنَّبِىُّ قُل لِّأَزْوَٰجِكَ إِن كُنتُنَّ تُرِدْنَ ٱلْحَيَوٰةَ ٱلدُّنْيَا وَزِينَتَهَا فَتَعَالَيْنَ أُمَتِّعْكُنَّ وَأُسَرِّحْكُنَّ سَرَاحًا جَمِيلًا ﴿٢٨﴾

Women may Attend Eid Prayers

Allah has honored all women and made them equal with man as to obligatory acts of worship. Women are encouraged to join public gatherings on Eid al-Adha and Eid al-Fitr, so that they may take part in these blessed prayers. This is also confirmed in a number of Hadith reported by Bukhari and Muslim, in which we see that the Prophet (peace and blessings be upon him) taught that all the women should come to these occasions. He said that even menstruating women should attend and take part in these blessed and joyous occasions. However, women should try to keep away from the prayer-place itself until the menstruation period is over. His concern that all women should attend the prayers was so great that he said that all women who had more than one jilbab (outer garment), should give a garment to her sister or neighbor who had none.

In this way he encouraged all women to attend Eid prayers and to do good and righteous deeds.

One day a good woman went to visit her sister at the castle of Banu Khalaf, and she narrated something from her sister. The sister's husband took part in a military campaigns with the Prophet (peace and blessings be upon him), and her sister also had accompanied her husband. The sister said: "We took care of the wounded." Her sister asked the Messenger of Allah (peace and blessings be upon him): "If a woman does not have a jilbaband (robe), then she cannot go to the Masjid?"

He (peace be upon him) said: "Let her friend or sister give her one of her jilbabs, so that she can come out and join the righteous gatherings."

Jabir ibn Abdullah said: "The Messenger of Allah (peace and blessings be upon him) led the prayer during Eid al-Fitr. Then he addressed the people. When the Prophet of Allah (peace and blessings be upon him) had finished his khutbah (sermon), he spoke to women, and then Bilal spread out his cloak for the women to put their sadaqah (donation) in it. Ibn Jurayj asked: "Was it zakat al-fitr?" He said: "No, it was the sadaqah." So a woman threw her ring into the cloak, then others did the same. According to this hadith, the Messenger of Allah (peace and blessings be upon him) accepted the sadaqah that they themselves willingly gave. This is shows the importance of congregational prayer for both men and women.

Although Islam does not force women to attend congregational prayer, women should still gather together at home, and offer the prayers in congregation.

In this case, the woman who is leading the prayer must stand in the middle of the (first) row, not in front. The women do not have to recite the adhan or the iqamah. This is what Umm Salamah, the wife of the Prophet (peace be upon him), did when she led women in prayer.

Women should try to Pray Sunnah and Nafil Prayer

Women must not limit themselves to the five daily obligatory prayers; they must try to pray Sunnah prayers as the Prophet (peace and blessings be upon him) did, and women must try to pray many of the nafil (supererogatory) prayers as their time and energy allow.

And keep constant vigil with it (The Qur'an) (part) of the night (These are the late night supererogatory prayers) as an accordance for you; it may be that your Lord will make you rise again to a praised station. (17:79)

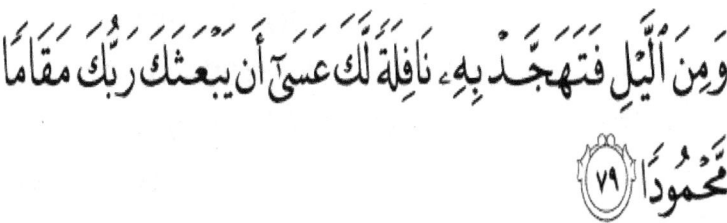

These prayers are salat al-duha, and Sunnah prayers following Maghrib, Isha, and prayers offered at night. Nafil prayers bring a person closer to God (Allah), and can earn them the love of Allah. There is no clearer words of the great status attained by a person who draws closer to Allah by praying nafil. On the authority of Abu Hurayrah (may Allah be pleased with him), who said that the Messenger of Allah (peace and blessing be upon him) said: Allah (mighty and sublime be He) said: Whosoever shows enmity to someone faithful, I shall be at war with him. When I love someone I am his hearing with which he hears, his seeing with which he sees, his hand with which he strikes and his foot with which he walks. And when My servants ask you, [O Muhammad], concerning Me - indeed I am near. I respond to the invocation of the supplicant when he calls upon Me. So let them respond to Me [by obedience] and believe in Me that they may be [rightly] guided. (2:186)

وَإِذَا سَأَلَكَ عِبَادِى عَنِّى فَإِنِّى قَرِيبٌ أُجِيبُ دَعْوَةَ ٱلدَّاعِ إِذَا دَعَانِ فَلْيَسْتَجِيبُوا۟ لِى وَلْيُؤْمِنُوا۟ بِى لَعَلَّهُمْ يَرْشُدُونَ ۝١٨٦

When Allah loves a slave, calls out the Angel Jibril and says: "I love so-and-so; so love that person." Then the Angel Jibril loves that person. After that, the Angel announces to the inhabitants of heavens that Allah loves that person; and so the inhabitants of the heavens also love him and then make people on earth love them too. Allah loves those who are constantly repentant and loves those who purify themselves. (2:222)

The Prophet (peace be upon him) used to pray a lot at night that his feet became swollen often. Aishah (May Allah be pleased with her) asked him: "Why do you do this, Messenger of Allah, when Allah has forgiven your sins, past and future?" He (peace and blessings be upon him) said: "Should I not be a grateful servant?"

The Prophet's wife Zaynab (May Allah be pleased with her) used to pray nafil prayers, and her prayers were long. One day she put up a rope between two column posts in the masjid, so that when she was tired, she can lean against the rope for a while. When the Messenger of Allah (peace be upon him) entered the masjid and saw the rope, he asked: "What is this the reason for the rope?"

The people answered: "It belongs to Zaynab. When she feels tired, she leans against the rope." He (peace be upon him) said: "Please untie the rope; let any of you pray as long as he/she has the energy, and if you feel tired, then please sit down."

A woman of Banu Asad, al-Hawla bint (daughter of) Tuwayt, used to pray all night, and she hardly ever slept. One day she visited Aishah when the Prophet (peace be upon him) was present. Aishah told him: "This is al-Hawla' bint Tuwayt. They say that she never sleeps at night." The Messenger of Allah (peace and blessings be upon him) said: "Please do only as much as you can, for by Allah, Allah never gets tired, but humans do."

The virtue of a deed that is done persistently, whether it be Qiyam al-Lail or anything else. The command to be moderate in worship, which means adopting what one can persist in. The command to the one who gets tired or weary when praying to stop until that feeling passes.

Aishah reported that the Messenger of Allah (peace be upon him) had a mat and he used it for making an apartment during the night and observed prayer in it, and the people began to pray with him, and he spread it (the mat) during the day time. The people crowded round him one night. He (the Holy Prophet) then said: O people, perform such acts as you are capable of doing, for Allah does not grow weary but you will get tired. The acts most pleasing to Allah are those which are done continuously, even if they are small. And it was the habit of the members of Muhammad's (peace be upon him) household that whenever they did an act they did it continuously.

Perform Prayers Properly

You must perform prayers properly, with deep concentration and precision. Think of the ayat (Quran) while reciting them, and the words of praise and glorification of Allah. Your soul should be flooded with fear of Allah, and with gratitude. If the devil happens to whisper something to you during the prayer, to distract you, try to focus more on the words that you are reciting from the Quran.

Do not rush back to your work when you finished praying. Rather, as the Prophet (peace be upon her) used to do, ask Allah for forgiveness by saying "Astaghfir-Allah" 3 times, and try to repeat the following dua:

*"**Allahumma anta al-salam**, **Wa minka al-salam**, **Tabaraka ya dha'l-jalali wa'l-ikram***

(O Allah, You are Peace and from You comes peace, Blessed are You,

O Lord of majesty and honour.)

Then repeat the adhkar and dua's that the Prophet (peace be upon him) used to recite after completing his prayer. There are many such adhkar, one of the most important of which is to repeat "***Subhan Allah***" 33 times, "***La ilaha ill-Allah***" 33 times, "***Allahu akbar***" 33 times, then to complete one hundred with "***La illaha ill-Allah wahdahu la shaika lah, lahu'l-mulk wa lahu'l-hamd, wa huwa `ala kulli shayin qadir.***"

According to a sahih hadith, the Prophet (peace and blessings be upon him) said: Whoever glorifies Allah (SWT) (says ***subhan Allah***) after every prayer 33 times, praises Allah (says ***al-hamdu lillah***) 33 times, and magnifies Allah (says ***Allahu akbar) 33 times***, which adds up to 99, then completes one hundred by saying *La illaha ill-Allah wahdahu la shaika lah, lahu'l-mulk wa lahu'l-hamd, wa huwa `ala kulli shayin qadir*, **their sins will be forgiven, even if they were as much as the sand of the earth**.

Then she turns to Allah humbly asking Him to correct all her affairs, in this world and the next one, and to bless her abundantly and to guide her in everything. And hold firmly to the rope of Allah all together and do not become divided. And remember the favor of Allah upon you - when you were enemies and He brought your hearts together and you became, by His favor, brothers. And you were on the edge of a pit of the Fire, and He saved you from it. Thus does Allah make clear to you His verses that you may be guided. (3:103)

وَٱعْتَصِمُوا۟ بِحَبْلِ ٱللَّهِ جَمِيعًا وَلَا تَفَرَّقُوا۟ وَٱذْكُرُوا۟ نِعْمَتَ ٱللَّهِ عَلَيْكُمْ إِذْ كُنتُمْ أَعْدَآءً فَأَلَّفَ بَيْنَ قُلُوبِكُمْ فَأَصْبَحْتُم بِنِعْمَتِهِۦٓ إِخْوَٰنًا وَكُنتُمْ عَلَىٰ شَفَا حُفْرَةٍ مِّنَ ٱلنَّارِ فَأَنقَذَكُم مِّنْهَا ۗ كَذَٰلِكَ يُبَيِّنُ ٱللَّهُ لَكُمْ ءَايَٰتِهِۦ لَعَلَّكُمْ تَهْتَدُونَ ﴿١٠٣﴾

The righteous woman finishes her prayers, purified in her heart. Allah will help her to cope with the burdens of life. Allah will make sure that she is not afraid nor sad. And Allah will guide her not to be miserly if she receives good fortune. (Humans are very impatient; they get upset when evil touches them; and they become very stingy when good fortune reaches them. And they become not so those devoted to Prayer. But those who remain steadfast to their prayer.

And those in whose wealth is a recognized right for the poor who asks and them who is prevented [for some reason from asking]) (70:19-25)

Righteous women must pay zakat on their wealth

Righteous women pay zakat. Each year at a specified time, women must estimate how much they own and must pay it. Zakat is not charity. It is a pillar of Islam, and there is no compromise or excuse when it comes to helping the needy and poor, even if you must pay thousands or even millions of dollars. The words of Abu Bakr (May Allah have mercy on him) concerning the people who refused to pay their zakat echo down the centuries to us: "By Allah I will fight whoever separates salat and zakat."

No woman can claim to be exempted because she is a woman. In Islam and in the eyes of Allah, women and men are equal. And they must pray and fast the same.

Righteous women fast during the day and pray as men do

Righteous women fast the month of Ramadan, and their soul is always filled with faith. O you who have believed, decreed upon you is fasting as it was decreed upon those before you that you may become righteous. (2:183)

$$\text{يَٰٓأَيُّهَا ٱلَّذِينَ ءَامَنُوا۟ كُتِبَ عَلَيْكُمُ ٱلصِّيَامُ كَمَا كُتِبَ عَلَى ٱلَّذِينَ مِن قَبْلِكُمْ لَعَلَّكُمْ تَتَّقُونَ ۝١٨٣}$$

Whoever fasts Ramadan out of faith and hope of reward, all their previous sins will be forgiven. So you should have the attitude of one who truly fasts, whose eyes and ears keep away from all kinds of sins that may diminish the reward. If a person finds themselves exposed to the trials of argument, then simply follows the Prophet's advice:

"When any of you is fasting, do not utter foul words and do not raise your voice in anger. If someone provokes you, just say, 'I am fasting as Allah commanded me.'" Whoever does not give up evil actions and false speech, then Allah has no need of them giving up water and food.

The reward for every good deed Allah will multiply between 10 and 700 times. However, fasting is different. Only Allah knows if you are truly fasting or not. Allah said: "Except for fasting, because it is for Me and I Myself will give payment for it." Then for everyone who fast, there are 2 * times of joy, at sunset when one eats, and one when they meet Allah. Allah told Prophet Moses (peace be upon him), the smell that comes from the mouth of one who is fasting is more pleasing to Me than the scent of musk.

The Prophet (peace be upon him) did more good deeds during Ramadan than at other times, especially during the last 10 days. Aishah (May Allah be pleased with her) said: "When the last 10 days of Ramadan began, the Messenger of Allah (peace be upon him) stayed up all nights and abstained from marital relations."

The Prophet (peace be upon him) asked Muslims to seek laylat al-qadr, and asked them to try to spend that night in prayer: "Seek laylat al-qadr during the last 10 days of Ramadan. Whoever worships Allah out of faith and hope of reward, all his previous sins will be forgiven."

The good woman helps her family to get up to eat suhur, in obedience to the command of the Prophet (peace be upon him). This is what the Prophet (peace be upon him) used to do and he taught his Companions too.

The benefits of marriage

When a servant of Allah marries, they perfect half their religion; and let them fear Allah in the remaining half.

Marriage in Islam is something positive for those that have reached the age of maturity. It should not never be delayed if there is a good partner available and also the means to establish a family.

Divorced people, widows, and widowers are encouraged to find someone and to re-marry. In Islam, religious celibacy is discouraged. Because it is very tough to control your physical desires even if you fast each day. Although marriage is not a compulsory duty, nevertheless, Islam favors marriage.

But do not marry polytheistic women until they believe. And a believing slave woman is better than a polytheist, even though she might please you. And do not marry polytheistic men [to your women] until they believe. And a believing slave is better than a polytheist, even though he might please you. Those invite [you] to the Fire, but Allah invites to Paradise and to forgiveness, by His permission. And He makes clear His verses to the people that perhaps they may remember. (2:221)

وَلَا تَنكِحُوا۟ ٱلْمُشْرِكَٰتِ حَتَّىٰ يُؤْمِنَّ وَلَأَمَةٌ مُّؤْمِنَةٌ خَيْرٌ مِّن مُّشْرِكَةٍ وَلَوْ أَعْجَبَتْكُمْ وَلَا تُنكِحُوا۟ ٱلْمُشْرِكِينَ حَتَّىٰ يُؤْمِنُوا۟ وَلَعَبْدٌ مُّؤْمِنٌ خَيْرٌ مِّن مُّشْرِكٍ وَلَوْ أَعْجَبَكُمْ أُو۟لَٰٓئِكَ يَدْعُونَ إِلَى ٱلنَّارِ وَٱللَّهُ يَدْعُوٓا۟ إِلَى ٱلْجَنَّةِ وَٱلْمَغْفِرَةِ بِإِذْنِهِۦ وَيُبَيِّنُ ءَايَٰتِهِۦ لِلنَّاسِ لَعَلَّهُمْ يَتَذَكَّرُونَ ۝

Prohibited to you [for marriage] are your mothers, your daughters, your sisters, your father's sisters, your mother's sisters, your brother's daughters, your sister's daughters, your [milk] mothers who nursed you, your sisters through nursing, your wives' mothers, and your step-daughters under your guardianship [born] of your wives unto whom you have gone in.

But if you have not gone in unto them, there is no sin upon you. And [also prohibited are] the wives of your sons who are from your [own] loins, and that you take [in marriage] two sisters simultaneously, except for what has already occurred. Indeed, Allah is ever Forgiving and Merciful. (4:23)

حُرِّمَتْ عَلَيْكُمْ أُمَّهَاتُكُمْ وَبَنَاتُكُمْ وَأَخَوَاتُكُمْ وَعَمَّاتُكُمْ وَخَالَاتُكُمْ وَبَنَاتُ الْأَخِ وَبَنَاتُ الْأُخْتِ وَأُمَّهَاتُكُمُ اللَّاتِي أَرْضَعْنَكُمْ وَأَخَوَاتُكُم مِّنَ الرَّضَاعَةِ وَأُمَّهَاتُ نِسَائِكُمْ وَرَبَائِبُكُمُ اللَّاتِي فِي حُجُورِكُم مِّن نِّسَائِكُمُ اللَّاتِي دَخَلْتُم بِهِنَّ فَإِن لَّمْ تَكُونُوا دَخَلْتُم بِهِنَّ فَلَا جُنَاحَ عَلَيْكُمْ وَحَلَائِلُ أَبْنَائِكُمُ الَّذِينَ مِنْ أَصْلَابِكُمْ وَأَن تَجْمَعُوا بَيْنَ الْأُخْتَيْنِ إِلَّا مَا قَدْ سَلَفَ إِنَّ اللَّهَ كَانَ غَفُورًا رَّحِيمًا ﴿٢٣﴾

And remember that day, when the hypocrite men and hypocrite women will say to those who believed, "Wait for us that we may acquire some of your light." It will be said, "Go back behind you and seek light." And a wall will be placed between them with a door, its interior containing mercy, but on the outside of it is torment. (57:13)

يَوْمَ يَقُولُ الْمُنَافِقُونَ وَالْمُنَافِقَاتُ لِلَّذِينَ آمَنُوا انظُرُونَا نَقْتَبِسْ مِن نُّورِكُمْ قِيلَ ارْجِعُوا وَرَاءَكُمْ فَالْتَمِسُوا نُورًا فَضُرِبَ بَيْنَهُم بِسُورٍ لَّهُ بَابٌ بَاطِنُهُ فِيهِ الرَّحْمَةُ وَظَاهِرُهُ مِن قِبَلِهِ الْعَذَابُ ﴿١٣﴾

Marriage is a relationship between a <u>man</u> and a <u>woman</u> that provides for the lawful development and expression of love. It links personal care with physical love and responsibility towards the partner and towards the sons and daughters that may be born of the union.

It is truly only in the context of marriage that women are protected for their vital role as mothers of the next generation. Modern experiments with free sex and single-parent families have confirmed the disruptive social and economic effects, more on women and their tragic effects for the next generation. Children of single-parent families are often more lost. They need both parents for a secure and well-adjusted life.

The benefit of marriage is important not only to the sons and daughters and wife, but also to the man.

Divorce causes suffering to the family, but also causes even more depression among men than women.

Women provide psychological comfort as well as physical love and should not be under-estimated.

Men without comforts of a wife and family are much more exposed to temptations of unlawful sexual relations and deviant unlawful behavior. It cannot be a mere coincidence that the decline of marriage in today's world has been accompanied by a rise in aggressive homosexuality, pornography, child abuse, murder, and rape - even of baby girls, boys, and old women. What is wrong with humanity? Have we forgotten the Quran or are we ignoring it? We will be questioned by Allah how we used our time. So let us use it wisely.

Zainab Ansari (Urdu: زينب أنصارى) was a six-year-old Pakistani girl who was on her way to a Quran recital when she was abducted. She was later found raped, acid thrown on her, and murdered. The perpetrator was identified as Imran Ali, who was determined to be a serial killer responsible for killing many young girls.

Nothing is hidden from Allah, on earth or in the heavens. In their hearts is disease, so Allah will increase their disease; and for them is a painful punishment. (2:10)

Allah has referred to the marriage as one of Allah's beautiful wonders. Marriage enshrines love, the greatest and most transforming of all human emotions. And of His signs is that He created for you from yourselves mates that you may find tranquility in them; and He placed between you affection and mercy. Indeed in that are signs for a people who give thought. (30:21)

وَمِنْ ءَايَٰتِهِۦٓ أَنْ خَلَقَ لَكُم مِّنْ أَنفُسِكُمْ أَزْوَٰجًا لِّتَسْكُنُوٓا۟ إِلَيْهَا وَجَعَلَ بَيْنَكُم مَّوَدَّةً وَرَحْمَةً ۚ إِنَّ فِى ذَٰلِكَ لَءَايَٰتٍ لِّقَوْمٍ يَتَفَكَّرُونَ ﴿٢١﴾

In another verse of the Qur'an Allah says: It has been made permissible for you the night preceding fasting to go to your wives [for sexual relations]. They are clothing for you and you are clothing for them.

Allah knows that you used to deceive yourselves, so He accepted your repentance and forgave you. So now, have relations with them and seek that which Allah has decreed for you. And eat and drink until the white thread of dawn becomes distinct to you from the black thread [of night]. Then complete the fast until the sunset. And do not have relations with them as long as you are staying for worship in the mosques. These are the limits [set by] Allah, so do not approach them. Thus does Allah make clear His ordinances to the people that they may become righteous. (2:187)

أُحِلَّ لَكُمْ لَيْلَةَ ٱلصِّيَامِ ٱلرَّفَثُ إِلَىٰ نِسَآئِكُمْ هُنَّ لِبَاسٌ لَّكُمْ وَأَنتُمْ لِبَاسٌ لَّهُنَّ عَلِمَ ٱللَّهُ أَنَّكُمْ كُنتُمْ تَخْتَانُونَ أَنفُسَكُمْ فَتَابَ عَلَيْكُمْ وَعَفَا عَنكُمْ فَٱلْـَٰٔنَ بَٰشِرُوهُنَّ وَٱبْتَغُوا۟ مَا كَتَبَ ٱللَّهُ لَكُمْ وَكُلُوا۟ وَٱشْرَبُوا۟ حَتَّىٰ يَتَبَيَّنَ لَكُمُ ٱلْخَيْطُ ٱلْأَبْيَضُ مِنَ ٱلْخَيْطِ ٱلْأَسْوَدِ مِنَ ٱلْفَجْرِ ثُمَّ أَتِمُّوا۟ ٱلصِّيَامَ إِلَى ٱلَّيْلِ وَلَا تُبَٰشِرُوهُنَّ وَأَنتُمْ عَٰكِفُونَ فِى ٱلْمَسَٰجِدِ تِلْكَ حُدُودُ ٱللَّهِ فَلَا تَقْرَبُوهَا كَذَٰلِكَ يُبَيِّنُ ٱللَّهُ ءَايَٰتِهِۦ لِلنَّاسِ لَعَلَّهُمْ يَتَّقُونَ ۝١٨٧

Comfort, protection and intimacy are all contained in the marriage relationship as it is intended to be. The Prophet (peace be upon him) said that: "You have seen nothing like marriage for increasing the love of two people."

Marriage is not a prison but a beautiful step, a safe sanctuary, a source of contentment, tranquility, comfort, and spiritual gift through shared commitment and experience.

If marriage is turned into an arena for conflict, discontent, oppression, or abuse, then it is failing to fulfill its proper role. Therefore every effort must be made to make sure that there is strong compatibility between a woman and a man before they are betrothed. Also, every effort must be taken to avoid the souring of a marriage once it is created.

Choosing the right partner

Marriages can go wrong very quickly if the couple are not compatible. Therefore, prevention in this respect is better than cure. It is very important to ensure that one is looking for the right qualities in a partner. The Prophet (peace be upon him) said: "A woman may be married for 4 reasons: (1) her wealth, (2) her rank, (3) her beaut, and (4) her religious character. Choose the woman with the religious character and prosper."

The same applies in the choice of a man by a woman. It is very foolish for a woman to choose a man because of his looks, wealth, or of high social status if he lacks good religious character. The first 3 are never a guarantee of happiness.

A man of genuinely religious character is most likely to understand and to observe the Islamic requirement of kindness to his wife and children, and to abide by Allah's laws with regard to his behavior towards everyone. His consciousness of Allah (swt) acts as a very strong restraint on his behavior. Whatever are his weakness, at least he does not deliberately try to do wrong.

Men and women should pray regularly for a good partner. They should also try to find out as much as possible about the character of the person. The Prophet (peace be upon him) advised us that a couple thinking of marriage must be given the chance to meet each other (in the presence of a relative) in order to determine at least basic compatibility.

Sincerity and trust

The Prophet (peace be upon him) said: "Religion is sincerity." A man asked: "Sincerity to whom?" Peace be upon him replied: "To Allah and His Book and His Messenger, and also to the leaders of the Muslims and to the generality of them."

Therefore, sincerity is strongly identified with true religious belief. Sincerity towards his wife, her husband, is an essential requirement for a husband and a wife. Firstly it implies having each other's interests at heart and wanting only good for each other. Secondly it implies truthfulness so that they learn to trust each other in word and deed. They would never tell each other a lie even in small matters because this will sow the seeds of doubt about trustworthiness in greater matters.

Once trust is gone, it is hard to rebuild it. If you tell a lie to cover up something else you did, this only compounds the offence. You should in all circumstances repent very sincerely to Allah (swt) and seek His forgiveness. You should then tell the truth and seek forgiveness unless the sin is a matter that could destroy the marriage. In such a case, you must repent to Allah silently and amend the behavior in future.

The Messenger of Allah (peace and blessings be upon him) directed people to forgive those who ask for forgiveness. The person who sincerely repents, tells the truth and seeks forgiveness may be able to re-establish trust. However, the shameless liar leaves the partner in a state of constant stress, doubt, and unworthy of trust. You must never throw away that basic trust for anything.

Another aspect of sincerity is supporting each other in doing what is lawful and avoiding what is wrong doing. Allah says: The believing men and believing women are allies of one another. They enjoin what is right and forbid what is wrong and establish prayer and give zakah and obey Allah and His Messenger. Those - Allah will have mercy upon them. Indeed, Allah is Exalted in Might and Wise. (9:71)

وَٱلْمُؤْمِنُونَ وَٱلْمُؤْمِنَٰتُ بَعْضُهُمْ أَوْلِيَآءُ بَعْضٍ يَأْمُرُونَ بِٱلْمَعْرُوفِ وَيَنْهَوْنَ عَنِ ٱلْمُنكَرِ وَيُقِيمُونَ ٱلصَّلَوٰةَ وَيُؤْتُونَ ٱلزَّكَوٰةَ وَيُطِيعُونَ ٱللَّهَ وَرَسُولَهُۥٓ أُو۟لَٰٓئِكَ سَيَرْحَمُهُمُ ٱللَّهُ إِنَّ ٱللَّهَ عَزِيزٌ حَكِيمٌ ﴿٧١﴾

This view on the acceptability of silence is based on comparison with a Hadith which allows for the use of a small "white lie." For example, someone that tried to reunite two people that were estranged:

"The person is not a liar when reconciling two people, and speaks good, and adds good from himself." (Hadith from Bukhari, Muslim, Tirmidhi, and Abu Dawud)

Heed unto Allah and His Messenger (peace and blessings be upon him). It is they upon whom Allah will bestow His mercy and grace: Indeed, Allah is the Merciful and Most Wise.

Both the husband and wife should be obedient and faithful to Allah and must help all the family to live a righteous life. There must always be mutual counselling within the family.

The Messenger of Allah (peace and blessing be upon him), long after the death his first wife, Khadijah, the Prophet always praised Khadijah for her loyalty and moral support during their married life together.

The husband and wife must trust each other. They must avoid suspicion and spying or snooping. The Quranic warning about these sins (49:12) is addressed in general to all believers, men and women. O you who have believed, avoid much [negative] assumption. Indeed, some assumption is a big sin. And do not spy or backbite each other. Would one of you like to eat the flesh of his brother when dead? You would detest it. And fear Allah; Allah is Accepting of repentance and Merciful.

يَٰٓأَيُّهَا ٱلَّذِينَ ءَامَنُوا۟ ٱجْتَنِبُوا۟ كَثِيرًا مِّنَ ٱلظَّنِّ إِنَّ بَعْضَ ٱلظَّنِّ إِثْمٌ وَلَا تَجَسَّسُوا۟ وَلَا يَغْتَب بَّعْضُكُم بَعْضًا أَيُحِبُّ أَحَدُكُمْ أَن يَأْكُلَ لَحْمَ أَخِيهِ مَيْتًا فَكَرِهْتُمُوهُ وَٱتَّقُوا۟ ٱللَّهَ إِنَّ ٱللَّهَ تَوَّابٌ رَّحِيمٌ ﴿١٢﴾

Negative assumptions are damaging. For example, if a husband senses that his wife is spying on him, he will lose the sense of security in his own home and could start to lock up his personal papers and effects. This may increase the wife's suspicions.

According to a Hadith the Prophet (peace and blessings be upon him) said that reading someone else's letters without permission is a sin. Wives may drive their husbands away by their snooping and spying. This will also be very distressing for the children to realize that the parents do not trust each other.

Understanding your husband

Most married couples only after marriage they become fully aware of each other's character, behaviors, tempers, likes and dislikes. There is always some period of adjustment after marriage. If all goes well, the honeymoon relationship grows into another dimension, a more mature love that is based on understanding of each other, but provided the partners do not behave so badly that they might kill the love altogether.

To cultivate this permanent and lasting kind of love, a wife must try to study her husband so as to know how to make him happy. In addition to knowing his likes and dislikes, a wife should also try to sense his moods and to respond to them, and to anticipate his desires. It is this responsiveness based on understanding and sympathy that creates strong bonds between the wife and the husband.

The Messenger of Allah (peace be upon him) said: "The world is a provision, and the finest provision of the world is to have a righteous wife." Peace be upon him also said: "Should I not tell you of the best treasure of man? It is a righteous wife: when she is near, she delights him; and when he tells her something, she is compliant; and when he is away from her, she looks after his interest."

In other words both have learned to respond to the needs of each other. And he loves her not by her physical beauty (which may fade) but by her loving actions and warmth. When he asks her to do something or not to do, she obeys with good will. She attends to his well-being and never hurts his feelings.

The husband is also comforted by the knowledge that his wife's concern for his well-being and welfare is not just a show but sincere. And she takes care of his business and interest when he is away. She also guards her chastity and honor when he is absent. All these are the characteristics of an ideal Muslim wife and woman. She has good manners and moral integrity.

There is another Hadith by the Prophet of Allah (peace be upon him) that describes the opposite behavior and its effects. For example, a woman that talks harshly and her husband becomes upset because of her rudeness. She gains the anger of Allah (swt) until she repents and tries to please her husband.

A woman that wants her marriage to last happily into old age must therefore learn these lessons.

Lover will never last forever if a woman is harsh, rude and disagreeable. Allah, the Almighty and Merciful, gives us a prayer in the Quran: And those who say, "Our Lord, grant us from among our wives and offspring comfort to our eyes and make us an example for the righteous." (25:74)

وَٱلَّذِينَ يَقُولُونَ رَبَّنَا هَبْ لَنَا مِنْ أَزْوَٰجِنَا وَذُرِّيَّٰتِنَا قُرَّةَ أَعْيُنٍ وَٱجْعَلْنَا لِلْمُتَّقِينَ إِمَامًا ﴿٧٤﴾

Authority and obedience

In every human group there is always a leader, a hierarchy of authority so that the members work together for the common good. The head of every family should be the oldest man, the husband, by virtue of his role as the protector of the family. Allah, the Most Merciful and the Mighty said: "Men are in charge of women by [right of] what Allah has given one over the other and what they spend [for maintenance] from their wealth. So righteous women are devoutly obedient, guarding in [the husband's] absence what Allah would have them guard. But those [wives] from whom you fear arrogance - [first] advise them; [then if they persist], forsake them in bed; and [finally], strike them. But if they obey you [once more], seek no means against them. Indeed, Allah is ever Exalted and Grand." (4:34)

ٱلرِّجَالُ قَوَّٰمُونَ عَلَى ٱلنِّسَآءِ بِمَا فَضَّلَ ٱللَّهُ بَعْضَهُمْ عَلَىٰ بَعْضٍ وَبِمَآ أَنفَقُوا۟ مِنْ أَمْوَٰلِهِمْ ۚ فَٱلصَّٰلِحَٰتُ قَٰنِتَٰتٌ حَٰفِظَٰتٌ لِّلْغَيْبِ بِمَا حَفِظَ ٱللَّهُ ۚ وَٱلَّٰتِى تَخَافُونَ نُشُوزَهُنَّ فَعِظُوهُنَّ وَٱهْجُرُوهُنَّ فِى ٱلْمَضَاجِعِ وَٱضْرِبُوهُنَّ ۖ فَإِنْ أَطَعْنَكُمْ فَلَا تَبْغُوا۟ عَلَيْهِنَّ سَبِيلًا ۗ إِنَّ ٱللَّهَ كَانَ عَلِيًّا كَبِيرًا ۝٣٤

Divorced women remain in waiting for three periods, and it is not lawful for them to conceal what Allah has created in their wombs if they believe in Allah and the Last Day. And their husbands have more right to take them back in this [period] if they want reconciliation. And due to the wives is similar to what is expected of them, according to what is reasonable. But the men have a degree over them [in responsibility and authority]. And Allah is Exalted in Might and Wise. (2:228)

وَٱلْمُطَلَّقَٰتُ يَتَرَبَّصْنَ بِأَنفُسِهِنَّ ثَلَٰثَةَ قُرُوٓءٍ ۚ وَلَا يَحِلُّ لَهُنَّ أَن يَكْتُمْنَ مَا خَلَقَ ٱللَّهُ فِىٓ أَرْحَامِهِنَّ إِن كُنَّ يُؤْمِنَّ بِٱللَّهِ وَٱلْيَوْمِ ٱلْءَاخِرِ ۚ وَبُعُولَتُهُنَّ أَحَقُّ بِرَدِّهِنَّ فِى ذَٰلِكَ إِنْ أَرَادُوٓا۟ إِصْلَٰحًا ۚ وَلَهُنَّ مِثْلُ ٱلَّذِى عَلَيْهِنَّ بِٱلْمَعْرُوفِ ۚ وَلِلرِّجَالِ عَلَيْهِنَّ دَرَجَةٌ ۗ وَٱللَّهُ عَزِيزٌ حَكِيمٌ ۝

This "level" of difference in legal rights in divorce and marriage is just a reflection of the husband's leadership role, and this in no way says that the woman is inferior. This point is stated by Allah, the Almighty and the Merciful: "Never will I allow to be lost the work of [any] worker among you, whether male or female; you are of one another. So those who emigrated or were evicted from their homes or were harmed in My cause or fought or were killed - I will surely remove from them their misdeeds, and I will surely admit them to gardens beneath which rivers flow as reward from Allah , and Allah has with Him the best reward." (3:195)

فَٱسْتَجَابَ لَهُمْ رَبُّهُمْ أَنِّى لَآ أُضِيعُ عَمَلَ عَٰمِلٍ مِّنكُم مِّن ذَكَرٍ أَوْ أُنثَىٰ ۖ بَعْضُكُم مِّنۢ بَعْضٍ ۖ فَٱلَّذِينَ هَاجَرُوا۟ وَأُخْرِجُوا۟ مِن دِيَٰرِهِمْ وَأُوذُوا۟ فِى سَبِيلِى وَقَٰتَلُوا۟ وَقُتِلُوا۟ لَأُكَفِّرَنَّ عَنْهُمْ سَيِّـَٔاتِهِمْ وَلَأُدْخِلَنَّهُمْ جَنَّٰتٍ تَجْرِى مِن تَحْتِهَا ٱلْأَنْهَٰرُ ثَوَابًا مِّنْ عِندِ ٱللَّهِ ۗ وَٱللَّهُ عِندَهُۥ حُسْنُ ٱلثَّوَابِ ﴿١٩٥﴾

The Messenger of Allah (peace be upon him) is also said: "All people (men and women) are equal, as equal as the teeth of a comb. And there is no claim of merit of a white person over a black person, or an Arab over a non-Arab, or a male over a female. Only God-fearing people merit a preference with Allah." All people are born equal, in the sense that no one brings any possession with him; and they die equal in the sense that they take back nothing of their worldly belongings. Allah judges every person on the basis of his own merits and according to his own deeds.

A woman should therefore acknowledge her husband's administrative leadership and should never dispute it, and must never set herself up as a rival in taking ultimate decisions that affect the family, even if she is the breadwinner, providing the largest portion to household income. A ship with two captains quarreling sinks, and the ship will never reach home. Still, leadership in Islam also has duties. The leader must always be motivated by love and concern for those people under his care, who will certainly respond by loving their leader.

The Messenger of Allah (peace be upon him) said: "The best of your leaders are those for whom you pray and who pray for you, and for whom you love and who love you, and the worst of your leaders are those whom you hate, and who hate you, and whom you curse and who curse you."

All forms of tyranny, cruelty, oppression and exploitation of the poor and weak are condemned, and tyrants are warned.

"You should fear the prayer of the oppressed, wronged, and persecuted, for truly there is no veil between them and Allah (swt). Tyrants shall never enter into Paradise."

The leader must consult his followers always. See the chapter in the Quran that is called "Shura", meaning consultation. "And those who have responded to their lord and established prayer and whose affair is [determined by] consultation among themselves, and from what We have provided them, they spend." (42:38)

وَٱلَّذِينَ ٱسْتَجَابُوا لِرَبِّهِمْ وَأَقَامُوا ٱلصَّلَوٰةَ وَأَمْرُهُمْ شُورَىٰ بَيْنَهُمْ وَمِمَّا رَزَقْنَٰهُمْ يُنفِقُونَ ﴿٣٨﴾

Leadership in Islam is recognized as a responsibility. It exists at several levels both in public issues and in the family. The Messenger of Allah (peace be upon him) said:

"Take care: everyone is a shepherd and each shall be asked concerning his flock. A leader is shepherd over his people, and he shall be asked concerning his flock. A man is a shepherd over everyone in his own house, and this man shall be asked concerning his flock. A woman is also a shepherd over her house and she shall be asked concerning her flock (husband, sons, and daughters). The servant is a shepherd over the property of his master, and the servant shall be asked about it. Each of you is a shepherd and each of you shall be asked about your own flock."

As can be read from this Hadith, the wife has a big role and responsibility within the family, running the household and raising the children. We shall return to this aspect of the wife's role in another section. In this section, we want to discuss the aspects of leadership and authority in the home. We want to also explain the use of the words "obeying" and "ordering" that are used in translating some Quranic verses.

The Arabic word "amr" has the meaning of "to ordain" or "to order". However, in the context of family life, "amr" clearly does not have the same meaning as in the army. The wife and the family are not a military unit, and for a man to shout out orders to his wife like a drill sergeant, would not be best, and definitely counter-productive.

The relationship of husband and wife is quite different. A healthy relationship is where the husband or wife does not need to hide or lie about money or property. If you cannot trust your life partner, then why marry them? A healthy relationship is where both husband and wife bring up their children equally. A husband and are described in the Quran but as "garments to each other," loving, sympathetic and protecting each other.

A study of the word "amr" in the Quran shows that it has many meanings, such as "biding," "commanding," "instructing" and "urging." For example in the Quran (2:168-9), Allah said: "O mankind, eat from whatever is on earth [that is] lawful and good and do not follow the footsteps of Satan. Indeed, he is to you a clear enemy. He gives you 'amr' only to do evil, and to commit deeds of abomination, and to attribute to Allah something of which you have no knowledge."

يَٰٓأَيُّهَا ٱلنَّاسُ كُلُوا۟ مِمَّا فِى ٱلْأَرْضِ حَلَٰلًا طَيِّبًا وَلَا تَتَّبِعُوا۟ خُطُوَٰتِ ٱلشَّيْطَٰنِ إِنَّهُۥ لَكُمْ عَدُوٌّ مُّبِينٌ ﴿١٦٨﴾

He only orders you to evil and immorality and to say about Allah what you do not know.

إِنَّمَا يَأْمُرُكُم بِٱلسُّوٓءِ وَٱلْفَحْشَآءِ وَأَن تَقُولُوا۟ عَلَى ٱللَّهِ مَا لَا تَعْلَمُونَ ﴿١٦٩﴾

How does Shaitan give 'amr' to people to do evil? Not by issuing commands but he whispers evil into the breasts of mankind. (114:5).

ٱلَّذِى يُوَسْوِسُ فِى صُدُورِ ٱلنَّاسِ ﴿٥﴾

Moreover, Allah that the Shaitan has no power over His creatures unless they choose to follow him. "My servants - no authority will you have over them, except those who follow you of the deviators." (15:42)

إِنَّ عِبَادِى لَيْسَ لَكَ عَلَيْهِمْ سُلْطَٰنٌ إِلَّا مَنِ ٱتَّبَعَكَ مِنَ ٱلْغَاوِينَ ﴿٤٢﴾

The Shaitan admits this. "Indeed, Allah had promised you the promise of truth. And I promised you, but I betrayed you. But I had no authority over you except that I invited you, and you responded to me. So do not blame me; but blame yourselves. I cannot be called to your aid, nor can you be called to my aid. Indeed, I deny your association of me [with Allah] before. Indeed, for the wrongdoers is a painful punishment." (14:22)

وَقَالَ ٱلشَّيْطَٰنُ لَمَّا قُضِىَ ٱلْأَمْرُ إِنَّ ٱللَّهَ وَعَدَكُمْ وَعْدَ ٱلْحَقِّ وَوَعَدتُّكُمْ فَأَخْلَفْتُكُمْ ۖ وَمَا كَانَ لِىَ عَلَيْكُم مِّن سُلْطَٰنٍ إِلَّآ أَن دَعَوْتُكُمْ فَٱسْتَجَبْتُمْ لِى ۖ فَلَا تَلُومُونِى وَلُومُوٓا۟ أَنفُسَكُم ۖ مَّآ أَنَا۠ بِمُصْرِخِكُمْ وَمَآ أَنتُم بِمُصْرِخِىَّ ۖ إِنِّى كَفَرْتُ بِمَآ أَشْرَكْتُمُونِ مِن قَبْلُ ۗ إِنَّ ٱلظَّٰلِمِينَ لَهُمْ عَذَابٌ أَلِيمٌ ﴿٢٢﴾

And so, it is clear that 'amr' does mean "to order" or "to command" in all contexts.

The word 'amr' then requires analysis and clarification according to its context. Then in the context of marriage, it may be understood to mean that the husband has authority as a leader in accordance with Islamic law.

The husband with gentleness should tell his wife what he wants to be done to enlist her assistance. Everyone with an understanding of relationships will realize that this manner of communicating has a positive effect and is much more effective than screaming out orders in an arbitrary uncaring and inconsiderate approach.

Therefore, when asked to do something in a considerate manner, a wife can offer advice if she has another suggestion, but if the husband is not swayed, the wife must accept his authority and should comply, unless what he wants is unlawful or contrary to the teachings of Islam.

Both men and women have a higher obligation of obedience to Allah (swt). The Messenger of Allah (peace be upon him) said: "No obedience should ever be accepted to a created being which is in disobedience to Allah, the Creator."

Often the breakdown of marriage is the feminist concept that "women and men are inherently of equal worth," and therefore the family can have two absolutely equal leaders, the wife and the husband.

If in the ensuing battle of wills, neither the husband or wife is ready to give way, so the result is will be divorce or separation, which will have negative results on the entire family, the sons and the daughters, and ultimately on the society at large. Righteous women most often understand that it is very natural for a husband to lead, provided that he leads in a wise and gentle manner.

It is one of the comforts of marriage for a wife to know that she does not have to take sole charge and responsibility for all decisions in the family.

Allah (swt) has created men and women equal in their essential dignity and human personhood, but different in function with male leadership in the home and in the family. Men and women complement one another and must never compete against each other. "But if a woman fears from her husband contempt or evasion, there is no sin upon them if they make terms of settlement between them - settlement is best. And present in [human] souls is stinginess. But if you do good and fear Allah - then indeed Allah is ever, with what you do, Acquainted." (4:128)

وَإِنِ ٱمْرَأَةٌ خَافَتْ مِنۢ بَعْلِهَا نُشُوزًا أَوْ إِعْرَاضًا فَلَا جُنَاحَ عَلَيْهِمَآ أَن يُصْلِحَا بَيْنَهُمَا صُلْحًا ۚ وَٱلصُّلْحُ خَيْرٌ ۗ وَأُحْضِرَتِ ٱلْأَنفُسُ ٱلشُّحَّ ۚ وَإِن تُحْسِنُوا۟ وَتَتَّقُوا۟ فَإِنَّ ٱللَّهَ كَانَ بِمَا تَعْمَلُونَ خَبِيرًا ﴿١٢٨﴾

The family and the home

Your home can be a beautiful oasis or a nightmare, depending on what you make of it. As the custodian of the home, the wife sets the tone and atmosphere of the household.

The wife is not required by Islamic law to clean and cook, but she still the manager and therefore is responsible for ensuring that these essential jobs are done. If the husband can afford a maid or three, then he should hire a maid to relieve his wife of such tiring labor.

However, if the husband cannot afford a maid, then the wife should contribute her own labor as a form of Sadaqah (charity) for which she will for certain receive a great reward from Allah (swt).

If you refuse to help your own family, then Allah says: "Perhaps his Lord, if he divorces you, would substitute for him a wife better than you - submitting to Allah, believing, devoutly obedient, repentant, worshipping, and traveling - [ones] previously married and virgins." (66:5)

$$\text{عَسَىٰ رَبُّهُ إِن طَلَّقَكُنَّ أَن يُبْدِلَهُ أَزْوَٰجًا خَيْرًا مِّنكُنَّ مُسْلِمَٰتٍ مُّؤْمِنَٰتٍ قَٰنِتَٰتٍ تَٰٓئِبَٰتٍ عَٰبِدَٰتٍ سَٰٓئِحَٰتٍ ثَيِّبَٰتٍ وَأَبْكَارًا ۝}$$

The wife who wants to keep the family happy and together must ensure that the home is a happy place to be in, physically mentally, and spiritually. The intelligent wife knows well the value of the personal touch around the house. She cooks and makes the house pleasant and filled with love. It is true that the way to a man's heart is through his stomach. Preparing good food has a very special blessing in Islam, whether it is for the family, a guest or for charity to the needy.

If a wife is very busy to cook each day, then whatever food she makes with her own two hands, will earn her love and appreciation.

Lost are those who slay their children, without knowledge, and forbid food which Allah hath provided for them, inventing (lies) against Allah. They have indeed gone astray and heeded no guidance. (6:140)

$$قَدْ خَسِرَ ٱلَّذِينَ قَتَلُوٓاْ أَوْلَٰدَهُمْ سَفَهًۢا بِغَيْرِ عِلْمٍ وَحَرَّمُواْ مَا رَزَقَهُمُ ٱللَّهُ ٱفْتِرَآءً عَلَى ٱللَّهِ قَدْ ضَلُّواْ وَمَا كَانُواْ مُهْتَدِينَ ﴿١٤٠﴾$$

Allah says: "Eat from the good food and work righteousness. Indeed, I know of what you do."

The management of the household is not her only duty, the wife is also responsible for the early education and care of the children. Breast-feeding is also very vital, because of its physical benefits and for establishment of a close bond between baby and mother. Breast-milk shields the child from illness, and it helps a child's intellectual growth. Allah recommends a long period of breast-feeding to maximize the benefits to the child: "And We have enjoined upon man, to his parents, good treatment. His mother carried him with hardship and gave birth to him with hardship, and his gestation and **weaning [period] is thirty months**. [He grows] until, when he reaches maturity and reaches [the age of] forty years, he says, "My Lord, enable me to be grateful for Your favor which You have bestowed upon me and upon my parents and to work righteousness of which You will approve and make righteous for me my offspring." (46:15).

وَوَصَّيْنَا ٱلْإِنسَٰنَ بِوَٰلِدَيْهِ إِحْسَٰنًا ۖ حَمَلَتْهُ أُمُّهُۥ كُرْهًا وَوَضَعَتْهُ كُرْهًا ۖ وَحَمْلُهُۥ وَفِصَٰلُهُۥ ثَلَٰثُونَ شَهْرًا ۚ حَتَّىٰٓ إِذَا بَلَغَ أَشُدَّهُۥ وَبَلَغَ أَرْبَعِينَ سَنَةً قَالَ رَبِّ أَوْزِعْنِىٓ أَنْ أَشْكُرَ نِعْمَتَكَ ٱلَّتِىٓ أَنْعَمْتَ عَلَىَّ وَعَلَىٰ وَٰلِدَىَّ وَأَنْ أَعْمَلَ صَٰلِحًا تَرْضَىٰهُ وَأَصْلِحْ لِى فِى ذُرِّيَّتِىٓ ۖ إِنِّى تُبْتُ إِلَيْكَ وَإِنِّى مِنَ ٱلْمُسْلِمِينَ ﴿١٥﴾

The mother's care and love is of lasting significance. Positive childhood imprints are important to develop healthy adults. The effects of the impressions of childhood remain throughout adult life. It is as "writing on stone"; its effects last forever.

A wise mother can use positive influence to nurture her children to be loving, kind, confident, considerate and thoughtful, disciplined, intellectually and spiritually awake and mindful of Allah in whatever they do.

An Arab proverb says: "The mother is the school, the fountain of knowledge, the world, and with such tender solicitude for the child's future does this first and best teacher impart her." This is not an empty compliment but an important observation which has implications for the importance of the mother's job. From the moment of birth a child seeks to connect himself with his mother. Even most cats and animals do that.

For many years the mother plays the most important role in his life. The child is completely (100%) dependent upon her. It is in this environment that awareness, and ability to comprehend and cooperate first develops. The mother gives her child the first interaction with another human being. The mother is truly his first bridge to social life. A child who is not able to make a connection at all with his mother, or with some other person who took her place, would certainly perish.

New situations happen each day. There are thousands of points in which a wife must apply her vision and understanding to her children's need. She can be very skillful only if she love her children and occupied in winning their affection and securing their welfare.

Human society is bound up with the attitude of a woman to motherhood. Women's part in life is often undervalued and treated as secondary. When the woman's part is undervalued, then the harmony of married life is destroyed.

If we can trace back the cases of failure in life, we would discover that the mother did not fulfil her function well. She did not give her children a good start. If the mother fails, if she is dissatisfied with her tasks and lack interest, then mankind is endangered.

Islam has recognized the value and importance of motherhood. A mother is given full appreciation for her work and for the pains that she endures, and for the sacrifices that she makes for the sake of her children. The Messenger of Allah (peace be upon him) said that Paradise lies at the feet of mothers." Peace be upon him also said that: "I and the mothers whose face have grown dark (worrying and carrying about their children) shall be like this on the Day of Resurrection." The Prophet (peace be upon him) placed together his middle and forefingers (meaning, that the mothers would be standing next to him).

A man asked the Prophet, who is the most deserving? The Prophet replied: "Your mother." The man asked: "And who after that?" Peace be upon him said: "Your mother." The man asked: "And who after that?" Peace be upon him repeated: "Your mother, then your father, then your nearest relatives in order of closeness."

The father is also very important in child upbringing. However, it is wrong to devalue the role of the mother. Humans are obsessed with paid employment and material gains and so often the role of the homemaker and the mother has come to be regarded as meaningless.

If a housewife or househusband is asked what they do (meaning their occupation) they likely to reply "Oh, not much at the moment. I stay at home and I take care of the children." Women and man have been brainwashed into thinking that a stay at home dad or mom is meaningless and demands no pay or special skill, and so their work is rated as zero in terms of occupational status and reward. For both women and men their home must not be their prison. Their home must be the center of their attention and their partner and children's welfare must be their first priority after their obligation to Allah.

This must not rule out them taking on a job outside the home, or continuing with their education, or volunteering and helping the community.

"Sallamah, the nurse of Ibrahim, the Prophet's son (before Ibrahim died), said to the Prophet (peace be upon him): O Messenger of Allah, you brought good news of all the good things to men but not to women." Peace be upon him said: "Did your women friends asked you to ask me this question?" Sallamah said: "Yes, they did."

Peace be upon him said: "Does it not please anyone of you that if she becomes pregnant and her husband is happy with her that she receives the reward of one who fast and prays for the sake of Allah? And when the labor and her pains come, no one in Heaven nor earth knows what is concealed in her womb to soothe her.

And when she delivers, not a mouthful of milk flows from her and not an instance of the baby's suck, but she receives, for every suck, the reward of a good deed. And if the baby kept her awake at night, she receives the reward of one who frees 70 slaves for the sake of Allah."

Acceptance of good advice

Leadership is defined as the process of influencing the activities of an organized group toward some goals. To achieve these goals, the leader must consult and accept good advice. And in a successful marriage good communication between husband and wife is important. Matters about the children's education, marriage, and other family affairs such as money, must be discussed for mutual agreement and understanding.

The wife must also be concerned about her husband's work and other activities, and should keep up-to-date about current affairs and general knowledge. For this it helps a great deal if there is a reasonable level of educational quality between the wife and her husband.

If the educational gap is too great, then the wife and husband will be unable to communicate effectively because her degree of understanding will be too low for her to share his interests and worries. So the husband and wife could drift far apart since they have nothing in common or of shared interest to discuss. In such cases the husband may devote most of his free hours outside the home with his workmates, and comes home only to eat, wash, and sleep. If the wife is so unlucky to have a low educational level, then she must remedy the situation, whatever her age.

The Messenger of Allah (peace and blessings be upon him) taught us that "the quest for knowledge is a duty for every person, female and male," and that it must be pursued and chased "from the cradle to the grave." The husband should try his best to support and to encourage her in every possible way.

By broadening her knowledge, a woman becomes a better and a more interesting companion, and will be in a far better position to advise her partner. Similarly if her religious education was neglected at an earlier age, she can take classes, or she can read more books. This can help teach her own children in turn.

The best role model for an intellectual woman is the Prophet's wife Aisha who engaged the Prophet (peace be upon him) in deep questioning about Allah until she was satisfied. As a result, Peace be upon him, advised people that they could learn from Aisha. Afterwards, when she became a widow, she became a noted authority on Hadith, and so her opinion was sought by many leaders on political, legal, and social issues.

The wife and husband, at the time of marriage, may come from dissimilar backgrounds, different cultural, different socio-economic background, or simply a different family way of life. They must not react with fear to such natural differences but must exercise acceptance and humor in the process of adjustment. In this way, with time, they will gradually come to a shared understanding and develop their own standards and sense of priorities. They will begin to think of themselves as ""we" instead of as two totally different and independent individuals.

Money

A very important topic that needs mutual understanding is money. Both husband and wife must support the family to the best of their abilities. If the wife does not work, then she must learn to live within the budget and show appreciation.

"If you possessed the treasure of the Mercy of my Lord (wealth, money, provision, etc.), then you would surely hold back (from spending) for fear of (being exhausted), and man is ever miserly!" (17:100)

قُل لَّوْ أَنتُمْ تَمْلِكُونَ خَزَآئِنَ رَحْمَةِ رَبِّى إِذًا لَّأَمْسَكْتُمْ خَشْيَةَ ٱلْإِنفَاقِ ۚ وَكَانَ ٱلْإِنسَٰنُ قَتُورًا ﴿١٠٠﴾

And enjoin prayer upon your family [and people] and be steadfast therein. We ask you not for provision; We provide for you, and the [best] outcome is for [those of] righteousness. (20:132)

وَأْمُرْ أَهْلَكَ بِالصَّلَوٰةِ وَاصْطَبِرْ عَلَيْهَا ۖ لَا نَسْـَٔلُكَ رِزْقًا ۖ نَحْنُ نَرْزُقُكَ ۗ وَالْعَـٰقِبَةُ لِلتَّقْوَىٰ ﴿١٣٢﴾

A woman must avoid the two extremes of meanness and extravagance as the Holy Quran states: "And [they are] those who, when they spend, do so not excessively or sparingly but are ever, between that, [justly] moderate." (25:67)

وَالَّذِينَ إِذَآ أَنفَقُوا۟ لَمْ يُسْرِفُوا۟ وَلَمْ يَقْتُرُوا۟ وَكَانَ بَيْنَ ذَٰلِكَ قَوَامًا ﴿٦٧﴾

A wife must avoid all wastefulness, which the Quran identifies as a lack of gratitude to Allah (swt).

Indeed, the wasteful are brothers of the devils, and ever has Satan been to his Lord ungrateful. (17:27)

إِنَّ ٱلْمُبَذِّرِينَ كَانُوٓا۟ إِخْوَٰنَ ٱلشَّيَٰطِينِ ۖ وَكَانَ ٱلشَّيْطَٰنُ لِرَبِّهِۦ كَفُورًا ﴿٢٧﴾

Both husband and wife must also avoid demands for luxuries. If woman is a good wife, a husband may take pleasure in surprising his wife with gifts from time to time. However, to constantly buy clothes, jewelry, and cosmetics, can cause even patient husbands to feel tired and angry.

Allah (swt) likes his servants to enjoy the lawful things, but in moderation. If man or woman has surplus it is best to give some of it away as sadaqah (charity) to people in need than to waste it.

If a wife earns money from anything, Allah (swt) gave her full rights over that income. However, if her husband is not well off, it is the best act of charity to support her husband and to contribute something to the family expenses.

It is therefore best for a wife and husband to talk about money matters always from the start of the marriage. In this respect the family must identify the priorities, the highest amongst which must be to save enough money for the best education for the children, which the Messenger of Allah (peace be upon him) described as the best gift one could make to their child.

Friendship

Before marriage a woman naturally has a circle of friends. These friendships are often for life and not let go on marriage, but a wife must remember that her closet friend should always be her partner, her husband. It is wrong to tell her friends the details of her married life, or to discuss the sexual relationship. It must always remain entirely private. She must never talk to anyone about what her husband says to her in a private conversation. It is reckless and could do harm if his private remarks become a source of gossip. If a wife cannot control her own tongue, she will lose her husband. If she wants to be her husband's ally, then she must always keep confidential matters to herself. "Do they not know that Allah knows what they keep secret and what they make known?" (2:77)

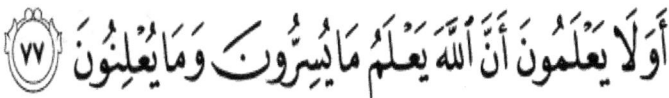

"Do they think that Allah hears not their secrets and their private conversations? Yes, [We do], and Our messengers are with them recording." (43:80)

$$\text{أَمْ يَحْسَبُونَ أَنَّا لَا نَسْمَعُ سِرَّهُمْ وَنَجْوَاهُم بَلَىٰ وَرُسُلُنَا لَدَيْهِمْ يَكْتُبُونَ ﴿٨٠﴾}$$

"Verily Allah knows the secrets of the heavens and the earth: and Allah Sees well all that ye do." (49:18)

$$\text{إِنَّ ٱللَّهَ يَعْلَمُ غَيْبَ ٱلسَّمَٰوَٰتِ وَٱلْأَرْضِ وَٱللَّهُ بَصِيرٌ بِمَا تَعْمَلُونَ ﴿١٨﴾}$$

And when the Prophet confided to one of his wives, but she told others of it and Allah showed it to him, he made known part of it and ignored a part. And when he informed her about it, she said: "Who told you this?" He said, "I was informed by the Knowing, the Acquainted." (66:33)

$$\text{وَإِذْ أَسَرَّ ٱلنَّبِيُّ إِلَىٰ بَعْضِ أَزْوَٰجِهِ حَدِيثًا فَلَمَّا نَبَّأَتْ بِهِ وَأَظْهَرَهُ ٱللَّهُ عَلَيْهِ عَرَّفَ بَعْضَهُ وَأَعْرَضَ عَنْ بَعْضٍ فَلَمَّا نَبَّأَهَا بِهِ قَالَتْ مَنْ أَنبَأَكَ هَٰذَا قَالَ نَبَّأَنِيَ ٱلْعَلِيمُ ٱلْخَبِيرُ ﴿٣﴾}$$

If there is ever an issue between her and her husband on which she needs advice, she must be very cautious, and must ask only a person of proven integrity, who will give her good and sincere counsel, and will never tell others.

In her public appearance, a woman must always observe Islamic codes of dress and behave modesty. She must not show off her figure, her clothes and her jewelry. She must also avoid wearing perfume in public. The perfume is only to attract her husband. Her dress must cover all parts of the body except her face and hands. It must not be tight nor transparent. It must not make her look like a man. The style and color is not important as long as the dress conforms to the Islamic values, and is not designed to attract men's attention. When she is in her own house, or away from the sight of men, she may dress in anything that she likes to please herself and her husband.

And tell the believing women to reduce [some] of their vision and guard their private parts and not expose their adornment except that which appears thereof and to wrap [a portion of] their headcovers over their chests and not expose their adornment except to their husbands, their fathers, their husbands' fathers, their sons, their husbands' sons, their brothers, their brothers' sons, their sisters' sons, their women, that which their right hands possess, or those male attendants having no physical desire, or children who are not yet aware of the private aspects of women. And let them not stamp their feet to make known what they conceal of their adornment. And turn to Allah in repentance, all of you, O believers that you might succeed. (24:31)

وَقُل لِّلْمُؤْمِنَٰتِ يَغْضُضْنَ مِنْ أَبْصَٰرِهِنَّ وَيَحْفَظْنَ فُرُوجَهُنَّ وَلَا يُبْدِينَ زِينَتَهُنَّ إِلَّا مَا ظَهَرَ مِنْهَا ۖ وَلْيَضْرِبْنَ بِخُمُرِهِنَّ عَلَىٰ جُيُوبِهِنَّ ۖ وَلَا يُبْدِينَ زِينَتَهُنَّ إِلَّا لِبُعُولَتِهِنَّ أَوْ ءَابَآئِهِنَّ أَوْ ءَابَآءِ بُعُولَتِهِنَّ أَوْ أَبْنَآئِهِنَّ أَوْ أَبْنَآءِ بُعُولَتِهِنَّ أَوْ إِخْوَٰنِهِنَّ أَوْ بَنِىٓ إِخْوَٰنِهِنَّ أَوْ بَنِىٓ أَخَوَٰتِهِنَّ أَوْ نِسَآئِهِنَّ أَوْ مَا مَلَكَتْ أَيْمَٰنُهُنَّ أَوِ ٱلتَّٰبِعِينَ غَيْرِ أُو۟لِى ٱلْإِرْبَةِ مِنَ ٱلرِّجَالِ أَوِ ٱلطِّفْلِ ٱلَّذِينَ لَمْ يَظْهَرُوا۟ عَلَىٰ عَوْرَٰتِ ٱلنِّسَآءِ ۖ وَلَا يَضْرِبْنَ بِأَرْجُلِهِنَّ لِيُعْلَمَ مَا يُخْفِينَ مِن زِينَتِهِنَّ ۚ وَتُوبُوٓا۟ إِلَى ٱللَّهِ جَمِيعًا أَيُّهَ ٱلْمُؤْمِنُونَ لَعَلَّكُمْ تُفْلِحُونَ ﴿٣١﴾

The wisdom behind the difference between a woman's public and private appearance

A woman's outer beauty is a part of her sexual appeal. And dress and adornment can either enhance that attraction or can conceal it. Allah requires a husband and wife to be faithful to each other, and He recommended punishment for adultery. It is a part of wisdom then to fear Allah and to wear clothes that conceal the body, so as not to encourage the very thing which Allah forbids. On the other hand, Allah does not regard sexual relations between spouses as sinful. On the contrary, Allah wants married partners to enjoy sexual relations with each other, since this will reduce temptations to seek satisfaction outside marriage. Therefore, women at home must take care of their appearance and should wear nice clothes, jewelry and perfume to enhance their attraction to their husband.

"O Prophet! Why do you forbid (yourself) that which Allah has made lawful for you; you seek to please your wives; and Allah is Forgiving, Merciful. ((66:1)

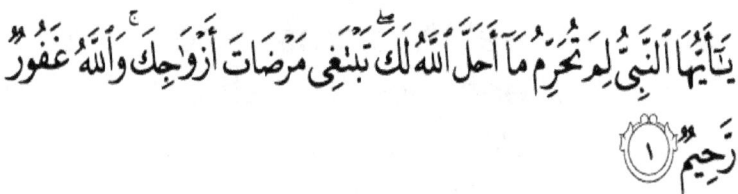

Most wives foolishly practice the reverse, they wear their most attractive clothes outside the house, in order to be admired by strangers, and when they are at home they wear their old and dirty clothes with untidy hair and appearance as if it no longer matters if their own husbands find them attractive or not. The Messenger of Allah (peace and blessings be upon him) said that all women may go out alone for their needs. However, provided they are in hijab (modest Islamic dress), then they may go out for any lawful purpose.

Women however must not roam around aimlessly and must not mix without cause with men. They should always tell their husbands where they are going and have their consent.

Women must also not put themselves in a situation where they are alone with men other than their husbands, fathers, or brothers (within the prohibited degrees of marriage).

Women must not allow into their homes men of whom Allah and their husbands would not approve, nor should they visit such men. There may also be women of whom the husband disapproves, maybe because of their bad habits of spreading gossip, or maybe because they interfere in the family's affairs, or because of other harmful influence.

Women must avoid situations or actions that could give rise to gossip about their conduct, or jealousy of their husbands, even if they have no bad intentions.

If a woman's appearance and behavior indicate that she is a faithful wife, she will gain the respect of her husband, other people and avoid unwanted attention. If the husband is certain of his wife's true respect and love for him, he will trust her always, and be spared from jealousy and suspicion. All these principles of conduct, strengths the marriage and the success of the family's life.

Other aspects of family and social life that a wife must observe are respect for her parents and her husband's family. She must also be a good mother and a kind neighbor.

Worship Allah and associate nothing with Him, and to parents do good, and to relatives, orphans, the needy, the near neighbor, the neighbor farther away, the companion at your side, the traveler, and those whom your right hands possess. Indeed, Allah does not like those who are self-deluding and boastful. (4:36)

۞ وَٱعْبُدُوا۟ ٱللَّهَ وَلَا تُشْرِكُوا۟ بِهِۦ شَيْـًٔا ۖ وَبِٱلْوَٰلِدَيْنِ إِحْسَٰنًا وَبِذِى ٱلْقُرْبَىٰ وَٱلْيَتَٰمَىٰ وَٱلْمَسَٰكِينِ وَٱلْجَارِ ذِى ٱلْقُرْبَىٰ وَٱلْجَارِ ٱلْجُنُبِ وَٱلصَّاحِبِ بِٱلْجَنۢبِ وَٱبْنِ ٱلسَّبِيلِ وَمَا مَلَكَتْ أَيْمَٰنُكُمْ ۗ إِنَّ ٱللَّهَ لَا يُحِبُّ مَن كَانَ مُخْتَالًا فَخُورًا ﴿٣٦﴾

And if any one of the polytheists seeks your protection, then grant him protection so that he may hear the words of Allah. Then deliver him to his place of safety. That is because they are a people who do not know. (9:6)

وَإِنْ أَحَدٌ مِّنَ ٱلْمُشْرِكِينَ ٱسْتَجَارَكَ فَأَجِرْهُ حَتَّىٰ يَسْمَعَ كَلَٰمَ ٱللَّهِ ثُمَّ أَبْلِغْهُ مَأْمَنَهُۥ ۚ ذَٰلِكَ بِأَنَّهُمْ قَوْمٌ لَّا يَعْلَمُونَ ﴿٦﴾

Allah, Merciful said: "Never will I allow to be lost the work of [any] worker among you, whether male or female; you are of one another. So those who emigrated or were evicted from their homes or were harmed in My cause or fought or were killed - I will surely remove from them their misdeeds, and I will surely admit them to gardens beneath which rivers flow as reward from Allah , and Allah has with Him the best reward." (3:195)

فَٱسْتَجَابَ لَهُمْ رَبُّهُمْ أَنِّي لَا أُضِيعُ عَمَلَ عَامِلٍ مِّنكُم مِّن ذَكَرٍ أَوْ أُنثَىٰ ۖ بَعْضُكُم مِّنۢ بَعْضٍ ۖ فَٱلَّذِينَ هَاجَرُوا۟ وَأُخْرِجُوا۟ مِن دِيَٰرِهِمْ وَأُوذُوا۟ فِى سَبِيلِى وَقَٰتَلُوا۟ وَقُتِلُوا۟ لَأُكَفِّرَنَّ عَنْهُمْ سَيِّـَٔاتِهِمْ وَلَأُدْخِلَنَّهُمْ جَنَّٰتٍ تَجْرِى مِن تَحْتِهَا ٱلْأَنْهَٰرُ ثَوَابًا مِّنْ عِندِ ٱللَّهِ ۗ وَٱللَّهُ عِندَهُۥ حُسْنُ ٱلثَّوَابِ ﴿١٩٥﴾

The sexual relationship

Marriage is much more than sex, but the sexual relationship is important. Because without a good sexual relationship, it is likely that the husband or wife could look somewhere else for love and emotional or physical fulfilment.

The husband and wife need to be kind and responsive to each other's needs and moods. Women (and indeed, men) frequently fail to understand and see the differences between female and male sexuality and so they offend each other. They should always make clear to one another what they dislike or like. The wife should take care of herself always and should make herself more attractive to her husband. Allah has encouraged the expression of love in the context of a lawful and spiritual relationship.

"Your wives are a place of sowing of seed for you, so come to your place of cultivation however you wish and put forth [righteousness] for yourselves. And fear Allah and know that you will meet Him. And give good tidings to the believers. (2:223)

نِسَآؤُكُمْ حَرْثٌ لَّكُمْ فَأْتُواْ حَرْثَكُمْ أَنَّىٰ شِئْتُمْ وَقَدِّمُواْ لِأَنفُسِكُمْ وَٱتَّقُواْ ٱللَّهَ وَٱعْلَمُوٓاْ أَنَّكُم مُّلَـٰقُوهُ وَبَشِّرِ ٱلْمُؤْمِنِينَ ۝

If a wife is not feeling well or has good reasons for not wanting sex, the husband must understand but she must not make a habit of refusing him. Women often underestimate the humiliation a husband feels if he is often rejected. The Prophet (peace and blessing be upon him) said: "When a woman who has been called to her husband's bed but she refuses, if he spends the night feeling bad, the angels will curse her until the morning."

This is very tough language, but it must be said. There is serious consequences of their constant refusal. Because a man who is frequently rejected by his wife will feel offended, frustrated, and depressed. This will cause big tension and problems in the marriage and can lead to divorce. A patient man often will not say or pursue unlawful gratifications somewhere else, but some men will search for satisfaction elsewhere, with a prostitute or mistress, or by taking another wife secretly.

An intelligent wife that loves her husband must therefore understand the possible consequences of her coldness and must give her husband all the love he wants. In a long Hadith from Sahih Muslim, it said that some of the Prophet's Companions noticed that rich people might get more reward from Allah because of their ability to give more charity. The Prophet (peace be upon him) said that Allah (swt) made other things to be given in charity.

For example, praising Allah, enjoining of good actions, forbidding of evil actions, and sexual relations. The Companions said: "When one of us fulfils his sexual desire will we have reward for that?" Peace be upon him said: "If a person does it unlawfully he would be sinning. Therefore, if he does it lawfully, with his wife, he will have a reward."

Therefore, if a wife satisfies her husband within the lawful framework of marriage and so protecting him (and herself) from unlawful acts, then not only this pleases her husband but this pleases Allah (swt) greatly. "It has been made permissible for you the night preceding fasting to go to your wives [for sexual relations]. They are clothing for you and you are clothing for them. Allah knows that you used to deceive yourselves, so He accepted your repentance and forgave you. So now, have relations with them and seek that which Allah has decreed for you.

And eat and drink until the white thread of dawn becomes distinct to you from the black thread [of night]. Then complete the fast until the sunset. And do not have relations with them as long as you are staying for worship in the mosques. These are the limits [set by] Allah, so do not approach them. Thus does Allah make clear His ordinances to the people that they may become righteous." (2:187)

أُحِلَّ لَكُمْ لَيْلَةَ ٱلصِّيَامِ ٱلرَّفَثُ إِلَىٰ نِسَآئِكُمْ ۚ هُنَّ لِبَاسٌ لَّكُمْ وَأَنتُمْ لِبَاسٌ لَّهُنَّ ۗ عَلِمَ ٱللَّهُ أَنَّكُمْ كُنتُمْ تَخْتَانُونَ أَنفُسَكُمْ فَتَابَ عَلَيْكُمْ وَعَفَا عَنكُمْ ۖ فَٱلْـَٔـٰنَ بَـٰشِرُوهُنَّ وَٱبْتَغُوا۟ مَا كَتَبَ ٱللَّهُ لَكُمْ ۚ وَكُلُوا۟ وَٱشْرَبُوا۟ حَتَّىٰ يَتَبَيَّنَ لَكُمُ ٱلْخَيْطُ ٱلْأَبْيَضُ مِنَ ٱلْخَيْطِ ٱلْأَسْوَدِ مِنَ ٱلْفَجْرِ ۖ ثُمَّ أَتِمُّوا۟ ٱلصِّيَامَ إِلَى ٱلَّيْلِ ۚ وَلَا تُبَـٰشِرُوهُنَّ وَأَنتُمْ عَـٰكِفُونَ فِى ٱلْمَسَـٰجِدِ ۗ تِلْكَ حُدُودُ ٱللَّهِ فَلَا تَقْرَبُوهَا ۗ كَذَٰلِكَ يُبَيِّنُ ٱللَّهُ ءَايَـٰتِهِۦ لِلنَّاسِ لَعَلَّهُمْ يَتَّقُونَ ۝١٨٧

The right to sex is of course reciprocal. The wife also has the same rights over her husband. It should also be mentioned here again that Allah wants you to have children. Allah, the Merciful, said: "So now have sexual relations with them, and seek that which Allah has ordained for you." (2:187)

Islam has not prohibited child spacing by science that do not have any harmful side effects, but if it is with mutual consent of wife and husband.

Jabir, a good Companion of the Prophet (peace be upon him), said that during the period when the Holy Quran was being revealed, people practiced contraception by Coitus interrupts (azl). Also known as the pull-out method, is a method of birth control in which a man, during sexual intercourse, withdraws his penis from a woman's vagina prior to orgasm.

Muslim added that the Prophet (peace be upon him) heard about Azl, but did not prohibit it. Abortion however is prohibited unless the mother's life is at stake. This applies also to forms of family planning which allow conception to take place but kill the embryo or prevent it from settling in the womb. Barrier methods such as the condom are closest to the hadith (i.e., azl). Natural methods such as checking body temperature to avoid sex round the time of ovulation are good alternatives.

Women and men should pay attention to personal cleanliness so as not to cause offence. The wife must always bathe, and she should use effective deodorants. She should also remove pubic hair and use pleasant perfume to please her husband.

A Co-wife (the other wife)

Under Islamic marital jurisprudence, a man can take up to four wives, so long as he treats them all equally. While it is true that Islam permits polygyny, it does not require or impose it: marriage can only occur by mutual consent, and a bride can stipulate that her husband-to-be not take a second wife. Likewise, since a bride's consent to marriage is required in Islam, a woman cannot be forced to accept the proposal of a married man. Monogamy is by far the norm in Muslim societies, as most men cannot afford to maintain more than one family, and many of those who can would rather do without the trouble. However, there are circumstances where the wife would accept the coming of a second wife, as it may be preferable to the available alternatives, and in some cases first wife may actually welcome it.

Likewise the new wife may decide that she would rather share the man that she loves than not to be with him at all. There may also be cases where the first wife is ill and is unable to have children. In such circumstances, the second wife, may in fact be the preserver and savior of the marriage and the family.

Everything depends on the attitude of the women themselves, and of course this also depends on the ability of the man to be fair and just always between his wives and the children. Allah (swt) has made it clear that the man who is not capable and able of doing justice must then only marry one woman. "And if you fear that you will not deal justly with the orphan girls, then marry those that please you of [other] women, two or three or four. But if you fear that you will not be just, then [marry only] one or those your right hand possesses. That is more suitable that you may not incline [to injustice]. (4:3)

$$\text{وَإِنْ خِفْتُمْ أَلَّا تُقْسِطُوا فِي الْيَتَامَىٰ فَانكِحُوا مَا طَابَ لَكُم مِّنَ النِّسَاءِ مَثْنَىٰ وَثُلَاثَ وَرُبَاعَ ۖ فَإِنْ خِفْتُمْ أَلَّا تَعْدِلُوا فَوَاحِدَةً أَوْ مَا مَلَكَتْ أَيْمَانُكُمْ ۚ ذَٰلِكَ أَدْنَىٰ أَلَّا تَعُولُوا ۝}$$

The Messenger of Allah (peace be upon him) also said that a man with more than one wife, who is not just and fair between them, Allah will raise him from the grave on the Day of Judgment with half of his limbs hanging off.

The "just and fair" towards wives includes the ability to provide for them equally, but not only in material terms, but also to give each wife a fair share of his attention and time, which must include marital (sexual) rights. The husband must also give each of his wives separate homes or quarters, as was the Sunnah of the Messenger of Allah (peace and blessings be upon him).

If the husband is doing his best to act justly towards all his wives, how should the ideal wife behave to make her family happy?

The wife should regard the new wife not as a rival but as a friend and a sister. She should be sympathetic, and must try to exercise self-control, understanding and try to avoid deliberate offences. If she takes the lead in trying to make the new wife happy it will be a great start towards developing friendship and a relationship of kindness between wives. The new wife must try to understand the fears of the first wife. For example, the fear of no longer being the queen of the household, the fear of being ignored or displaced. Such fears, and possible envy if the new wife is more beautiful and younger, are natural human behavior and reactions, and can be calmed if the new wife is kind and uses her initiative to soothe them.

The wives should try to be helpful to one another, and cooperating in the smooth running of the households. If one wife is ill, the other should try to help as much as possible. If one travels or has a job, the other should look after the children. Try to exchange of gifts from time to time to sustain a kindly relationship. A wife must also be kind to her co-wife's children and to treat them like her own children. She must encourage her own children to be best friends with their half-brothers and sisters. Moreover, a wife must never try to poison her husband's mind against her co-wife or her children. If there is any friction between the wives, they must try to resolve the matter as sisters do.

If the man is fair and understanding, a polygamous marriage can be a happy life for all those involved, which has many advantages over the alternative options of divorce or unlawful sexual relationship outside marriage.

"And those who say, "Our Lord, grant us from among our wives and offspring comfort to our eyes and make us an example for the righteous." (25:74)

$$\text{وَٱلَّذِينَ يَقُولُونَ رَبَّنَا هَبْ لَنَا مِنْ أَزْوَٰجِنَا وَذُرِّيَّٰتِنَا قُرَّةَ أَعْيُنٍ وَٱجْعَلْنَا لِلْمُتَّقِينَ إِمَامًا ۝}$$

"O Prophet, say to your wives, "If you should desire the worldly life and its adornment, then come, I will provide for you and give you a gracious release." (33:280

$$\text{يَٰٓأَيُّهَا ٱلنَّبِيُّ قُل لِّأَزْوَٰجِكَ إِن كُنتُنَّ تُرِدْنَ ٱلْحَيَوٰةَ ٱلدُّنْيَا وَزِينَتَهَا فَتَعَالَيْنَ أُمَتِّعْكُنَّ وَأُسَرِّحْكُنَّ سَرَاحًا جَمِيلًا ۝}$$

The unreasonable husband

Some women are very unfortunate. Their men fail to follow the Prophet's Sunnah. Instead their husbands indulge in various sins that have very adverse effects on the marriage, on the family, and the children.

Under such circumstances the wife must try to guide and to advise him tactfully but very firmly, not by nagging or fighting but in a peaceful heart-to-heart talk, but if the husband's response is very negative or aggressive, she must seek the help of relatives. If that is not possible, then his friends, or a respected Imam (religious scholar) in persuading him to fear Allah, and to behave in a responsible manner. If this fails, then she it is best to take this matter to a Shari'ah court. If the husband is found guilty of offences that violate the requirements of marriage, the wife must be granted a divorce by the court.

"And if a woman fears from her husband contempt or evasion, there is no sin upon them if they make terms of settlement between them - and settlement is best. And present in [human] souls is stinginess. But if you do good and fear Allah - then indeed Allah is ever, with what you do, Acquainted." (4:128)

وَإِنِ ٱمْرَأَةٌ خَافَتْ مِنْ بَعْلِهَا نُشُوزًا أَوْ إِعْرَاضًا فَلَا جُنَاحَ عَلَيْهِمَا أَن يُصْلِحَا بَيْنَهُمَا صُلْحًا وَٱلصُّلْحُ خَيْرٌ وَأُحْضِرَتِ ٱلْأَنفُسُ ٱلشُّحَّ وَإِن تُحْسِنُوا۟ وَتَتَّقُوا۟ فَإِنَّ ٱللَّهَ كَانَ بِمَا تَعْمَلُونَ خَبِيرًا ﴿١٢٨﴾

If the wife does not have enough legal help, or evidence, or witnesses of her husband's misbehavior, then she should decide to request for Khul (a divorce by mutual agreement with the husband on the return of the dowry).

Allah, the Merciful says in the Quran: "And if he has divorced her [for the third time], then she is not lawful to him afterward until [after] she marries a husband other than him. And if the latter husband divorces her [or dies], there is no blame upon the woman and her former husband for returning to each other if they think that they can keep [within] the limits of Allah . These are the limits of Allah, which He makes clear to a people who know."

فَإِن طَلَّقَهَا فَلَا تَحِلُّ لَهُۥ مِنۢ بَعْدُ حَتَّىٰ تَنكِحَ زَوْجًا غَيْرَهُۥ ۗ فَإِن طَلَّقَهَا فَلَا جُنَاحَ عَلَيْهِمَآ أَن يَتَرَاجَعَآ إِن ظَنَّآ أَن يُقِيمَا حُدُودَ ٱللَّهِ ۗ وَتِلْكَ حُدُودُ ٱللَّهِ يُبَيِّنُهَا لِقَوْمٍ يَعْلَمُونَ ۝

Divorce is very disliked in Islam, and the Messenger of Allah (peace be upon him) warned us against it: "The tasters-male and female," i.e. those who repeatedly marry and divorce exchanging one partner after another.

Peace be upon him also said: "Of all the things Allah (swt) has made lawful, what Allah most hates is divorce."

The Prophet (peace be upon him) said: "If a wife asks her husband for a divorce without a strong reason for it, the scent of paradise will be forbidden to her forever."

Nonetheless divorce is still available in the final if a marriage is very harmful to the wife, and there is happiness or peace of mind to either of them.

If the wife for some reason does not want to divorce her husband in spite of his sins and misbehavior, she must be careful to avoid becoming his accomplice in his sins and evil-doings.

Allah, the Merciful, said: "Men are the protectors and maintainers of women. Righteous women are devoutly obedient (to Allah and to their husbands), and guard in the husband's absence what Allah orders them to guard (e.g. their chastity, their husband's property, etc.). As to those women on whose part you see ill-conduct, admonish them (first), (next), refuse to share their beds, (and last) beat them (lightly, if it is useful), but if they return to obedience, seek not against them means (of annoyance). Surely, Allah is Ever Most High, Most Great." (4:34)

ٱلرِّجَالُ قَوَّٰمُونَ عَلَى ٱلنِّسَآءِ بِمَا فَضَّلَ ٱللَّهُ بَعْضَهُمْ عَلَىٰ بَعْضٍ وَبِمَآ أَنفَقُوا۟ مِنْ أَمْوَٰلِهِمْ ۚ فَٱلصَّٰلِحَٰتُ قَٰنِتَٰتٌ حَٰفِظَٰتٌ لِّلْغَيْبِ بِمَا حَفِظَ ٱللَّهُ ۚ وَٱلَّٰتِى تَخَافُونَ نُشُوزَهُنَّ فَعِظُوهُنَّ وَٱهْجُرُوهُنَّ فِى ٱلْمَضَاجِعِ وَٱضْرِبُوهُنَّ ۖ فَإِنْ أَطَعْنَكُمْ فَلَا تَبْغُوا۟ عَلَيْهِنَّ سَبِيلًا ۗ إِنَّ ٱللَّهَ كَانَ عَلِيًّا كَبِيرًا ﴿٣٤﴾

"O you who have believed, obey Allah and His Messenger and do not turn from him while you hear [his order]." (8:20)

يَٰٓأَيُّهَا ٱلَّذِينَ ءَامَنُوٓا۟ أَطِيعُوا۟ ٱللَّهَ وَرَسُولَهُۥ وَلَا تَوَلَّوْا۟ عَنْهُ وَأَنتُمْ تَسْمَعُونَ ۞

"And obey Allah and His Messenger, and do not dispute and [thus] lose courage and [then] your strength would depart; and be patient. Indeed, Allah is with the patient." (8:46)

وَأَطِيعُوا۟ ٱللَّهَ وَرَسُولَهُۥ وَلَا تَنَٰزَعُوا۟ فَتَفْشَلُوا۟ وَتَذْهَبَ رِيحُكُمْ وَٱصْبِرُوٓا۟ إِنَّ ٱللَّهَ مَعَ ٱلصَّٰبِرِينَ ۞

This means that everyone is responsible for their own actions, and cannot push off the blame for their own sins on another person or their husband. If the husband is for example a drunkard, then she must never join in his drinking or buy him or serve him beer etc., even if he threatens her or orders her to do it.

This is in accordance to the Messenger of Allah (peace be upon him). There must never be obedience to a created being in disobedience to the Creator, Allah (swt). If your husband tries to force you to join him in wrong doing you should ask for a divorce, and a Shari'ah judges are bound under such circumstances to approve the divorce. This follows the same rules as the duty of Hijrah (Migration) for a Muslim if she or he is prohibited from practicing the essentials (pillars) of Islam. Anyone who decides to stay in a place where they are likely to lose their faith and become a part of a corrupt group will be asked by Allah (swt) on the Day of Judgment why they did not migrate to a land where they would have been able to practice their faith. "Indeed, those whom the angels take in death while wronging themselves - [the angels] will say, "In what [condition] were you?" They will say, "We were oppressed in the land." The angels will say, "Was not the earth of Allah spacious [enough] for you to emigrate therein?"

For those, their refuge is Hell - and evil it is as a destination." (4:97)

$$إِنَّ ٱلَّذِينَ تَوَفَّىٰهُمُ ٱلْمَلَٰٓئِكَةُ ظَالِمِىٓ أَنفُسِهِمْ قَالُوا۟ فِيمَ كُنتُمْ ۖ قَالُوا۟ كُنَّا مُسْتَضْعَفِينَ فِى ٱلْأَرْضِ ۚ قَالُوٓا۟ أَلَمْ تَكُنْ أَرْضُ ٱللَّهِ وَٰسِعَةً فَتُهَاجِرُوا۟ فِيهَا ۚ فَأُو۟لَٰٓئِكَ مَأْوَىٰهُمْ جَهَنَّمُ ۖ وَسَآءَتْ مَصِيرًا ﴿٩٧﴾$$

In the same way the ideal woman who has an un-Islamic husband must:

(a) Abstain from following and supporting him in wrongdoing;

(b) Advise him against his wrong-doing.

(c) Seek divorce if the only alternative is to be pulled into sin.

An example of one such woman is Asiya bint Muzahim who attained perfect faith as described by the Prophet (may the blessings and peace of Allah be upon him).

Asiya lived in ancient Egypt during the rule of the most oppressive pharaoh in history. Not only did she live under his rule, but she lived in his home as his wife. The pharaoh was a horrible tyrant who claimed to be an all-powerful god, and he made his people worship him. At the same time, however, he was so paranoid of being overthrown (as a fortune teller predicted) that he ordered baby boys born in the land to be killed. In one particular year, the newborn boys could live, and in the next, the newborn boys were killed. It was against this backdrop that Prophet Musa (Moses) (peace be upon him) was born, in a year the baby boys were to be killed. Asiya loved Musa as her own son. When he started preaching the message of the one true God, she believed wholeheartedly. However, being the wife of the violent and oppressive man who thought himself to be a god, she kept her faith secret.

Many men reached perfection but none among the women reached perfection except Mary, the daughter of Imran, the mother of Isa (Jesus) (peace be upon him), and Asiya, Pharaoh's wife. And the superiority of Aisha to other women is like the superiority of Tharid to other kinds of food. According to Hadith, Asiya will be among the first women to enter Paradise. Allah mentions Asiya as an example to all Muslims.

"And Allah presents an example of those who believed: the wife of Pharaoh, when she said, "My Lord, build for me near You a house in Paradise and save me from Pharaoh and his deeds and save me from the wrongdoing people." (66:11)

وَضَرَبَ ٱللَّهُ مَثَلًا لِّلَّذِينَ ءَامَنُوا ٱمْرَأَتَ فِرْعَوْنَ إِذْ قَالَتْ رَبِّ ٱبْنِ لِي عِندَكَ بَيْتًا فِي ٱلْجَنَّةِ وَنَجِّنِي مِن فِرْعَوْنَ وَعَمَلِهِ وَنَجِّنِي مِنَ ٱلْقَوْمِ ٱلظَّٰلِمِينَ ﴿١١﴾

If the wife is not able to get a divorce or cannot break free from the bad husband, then she should take comfort from the Quran verse which says: "Allah does not charge a soul except [with that within] its capacity. It will have [the consequence of] what [good] it has gained, and it will bear [the consequence of] what [evil] it has earned. "Our Lord, do not impose blame upon us if we have forgotten or erred. Our Lord, and lay not upon us a burden like that which You laid upon those before us. Our Lord, and burden us not with that which we have no ability to bear. And pardon us; and forgive us; and have mercy upon us. You are our protector, so give us victory over the disbelieving people." (2:286)

لَا يُكَلِّفُ ٱللَّهُ نَفْسًا إِلَّا وُسْعَهَا ۚ لَهَا مَا كَسَبَتْ وَعَلَيْهَا مَا ٱكْتَسَبَتْ ۗ رَبَّنَا لَا تُؤَاخِذْنَا إِن نَّسِينَا أَوْ أَخْطَأْنَا ۚ رَبَّنَا وَلَا تَحْمِلْ عَلَيْنَا إِصْرًا كَمَا حَمَلْتَهُۥ عَلَى ٱلَّذِينَ مِن قَبْلِنَا ۚ رَبَّنَا وَلَا تُحَمِّلْنَا مَا لَا طَاقَةَ لَنَا بِهِۦ ۖ وَٱعْفُ عَنَّا وَٱغْفِرْ لَنَا وَٱرْحَمْنَا ۚ أَنتَ مَوْلَىٰنَا فَٱنصُرْنَا عَلَى ٱلْقَوْمِ ٱلْكَٰفِرِينَ ﴿٢٨٦﴾

Therefore, in her very difficult situation she should avoid his sins in accordance with another Hadith:

"If any of you sees wrongdoing they must correct it with their hand, and if that is not possible they must correct it with their tongue, and if that is not possible they should hate it within their heart, and that is the weakest of faith."

On that tough day, the Day of Judgment, every man, woman, husband, and wife will stand alone, and Allah knows best what is in their heart.

You, your family, and Allah (swt)

You must understand that there are three parties to any marriage: the husband, the wife, and Allah, the Creator and Lord of everyone, who is always a witness. The Quran repeatedly gives a reminder that "Allah sees and hears everything." "And establish prayer and give zakah, and whatever good you put forward for yourselves - you will find it with Allah. (2:110)

وَأَقِيمُوا۟ ٱلصَّلَوٰةَ وَءَاتُوا۟ ٱلزَّكَوٰةَ وَمَا تُقَدِّمُوا۟ لِأَنفُسِكُم مِّنْ خَيْرٍ تَجِدُوهُ عِندَ ٱللَّهِ إِنَّ ٱللَّهَ بِمَا تَعْمَلُونَ بَصِيرٌ ﴿١١٠﴾

And do not make [your oath by] Allah an excuse against being righteous and fearing Allah and making peace among people. Allah is Hears and Knows all. (2:224)

Husband and wife should always help one another to live as good people, in voluntary submission to Allah (swt), and in obedience to what He has revealed through His Prophets (peace be upon them). The submissiveness of the wife to the husband is only as a recognition of the husband's position as the head of the family, and not in a servile bond, but as a respect to him.

Allah presents an example of those who disbelieved: the wife of Noah and the wife of Lot. They were under two of Our righteous servants but betrayed them, so those prophets did not avail them from Allah at all, and it was said, "Enter the Fire with those who enter." (66:10)

ضَرَبَ ٱللَّهُ مَثَلًا لِّلَّذِينَ كَفَرُوا۟ ٱمْرَأَتَ نُوحٍ وَٱمْرَأَتَ لُوطٍ كَانَتَا تَحْتَ عَبْدَيْنِ مِنْ عِبَادِنَا صَـٰلِحَيْنِ فَخَانَتَاهُمَا فَلَمْ يُغْنِيَا عَنْهُمَا مِنَ ٱللَّهِ شَيْـًٔا وَقِيلَ ٱدْخُلَا ٱلنَّارَ مَعَ ٱلدَّٰخِلِينَ ﴿١٠﴾

In the family, the husband should be a responsible leader, and his wife should be a responsible follower. If he is doing wrong she should tell him, and if she is doing wrong, he should tell her. Both must respond by trying to avoid repeating it. The Prophet (peace be upon him) said: "Paradise is the reward for a woman who pleases her husband until death."

A wife should try to avoid any behavior that is harmful to her family's welfare in this world or the hereafter, indirectly or directly. Allah (swt) warns: "O you who have believed, indeed, among your wives and your children are enemies to you, so beware of them. But if you pardon and overlook and forgive - then indeed, Allah is Forgiving and Merciful." (64:14)

يَٰٓأَيُّهَا ٱلَّذِينَ ءَامَنُوٓاْ إِنَّ مِنْ أَزْوَٰجِكُمْ وَأَوْلَٰدِكُمْ عَدُوًّا لَّكُمْ فَٱحْذَرُوهُمْ وَإِن تَعْفُواْ وَتَصْفَحُواْ وَتَغْفِرُواْ فَإِنَّ ٱللَّهَ غَفُورٌ رَّحِيمٌ ۝

The wife should try to be an asset to her family and never a liability. She should encourage everyone in doing good and discourage them from doing wrong.

She must never enter marriage with the intention of hunting for what she can get out of it in terms of money and material benefits. A good wife will find happiness and peace of mind corresponding to the devotion and commitment she puts into the marriage. To feel that her own family values and needs her is the true measure of success. A person is urged to be very merciful and forgiving towards others, as she or he hopes for Allah's forgiveness and mercy on the Last Day. A wife should therefore forgive any wrongs that were done in the past, and must not continue to rake up old grievances. "Kind words and forgiving of faults are better than Sadaqah (charity) followed by injury. And Allah is Rich (Free of all wants) and He is Most-Forbearing." (2:263)

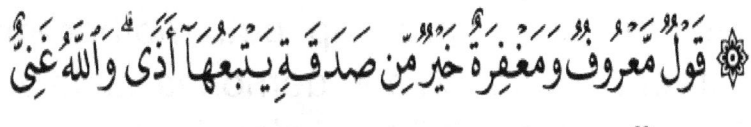

The family must try to find time always to read the Quran and Hadith together. This will help them to understand the laws of Allah and to live by them in their daily life, thereby increasing their faith.

Allah instructs and warns you concerning your children. The mother is always the first school. She must be fair, loving, and affectionate to all her children. She must direct them towards what is good and away from what is unlawful. The Prophet (peace be upon him) said: "Be generous to all your children, and excel in teaching them the best of manners and conduct." Ibn Umar reported the Prophet (peace be upon him) said: "What does a mother and father leave as an inheritance for their sons and daughters (that is) better than good morals?"

As the children grow up, both mother and father must teach and demonstrate Islam by example. Children also love stories and can benefit from those which have a moral message. Read to them *Stories of the Prophets*. Teach them about the last Prophet (peace be upon him). Teach them about Noah's (Nuh) (peace be upon him) faith, and the ark that saved Noah and his family from the flood. If it is prayer time the mother and father should call the children and pray together. After prayer, the parents can spend a few minutes explaining the Quranic verses so that the children over the years grow up with a broad knowledge of the teachings of Islam. As the children grow bigger the discussions can be extended further by reading from the *Quran*, *Hadith*, *Seerah of Prophet Muhammad* (biography of the Prophet, peace be upon him) and many other books that encourages the young child to realize Islam as the guiding force in his or her life.

"Our Lord, and send among them a messenger from themselves who will recite to them Your verses and teach them the Book and wisdom and purify them. Indeed, You are the Exalted in Might, the Wise." (2:129)

رَبَّنَا وَابْعَثْ فِيهِمْ رَسُولًا مِنْهُمْ يَتْلُواْ عَلَيْهِمْ ءَايَٰتِكَ وَيُعَلِّمُهُمُ ٱلْكِتَٰبَ وَٱلْحِكْمَةَ وَيُزَكِّيهِمْ ۚ إِنَّكَ أَنتَ ٱلْعَزِيزُ ٱلْحَكِيمُ ۝

You are that messenger to your children. In this way your children insha' Allah (if God wills) will grow up and become a source of comfort and joy to the parents. The Messenger of Allah (peace be upon him) said that leaving behind good and righteous sons and daughters who will pray for their parents is a Sadaqatun Jariatan (continuous charity) that will bring great blessings to the parents even after their death.

This is the religion of the Messenger of Allah (peace and blessings be upon him). Islam teaches good will and compassion to all creatures. The ideal Muslim woman must never be in competition with her family or husband. Her soul was created by Allah, so that proves that her soul is her husband's equal. But in any marriage a woman's role is complementary to that of her husband. Her responsibilities and duties are not the same as his. She can fulfil her responsibilities by putting aside her selfish desires and wants. She must understand that her family is always her first priority after her duty to Allah.

The Messenger of Allah (peace be upon him) said: "If I had ordered that anyone should prostrate before another, I would have ordered that a wife should prostrate before her husband."

However, such prostration, submission, to a human being would constitute shirk (associating someone with Allah (swt) in worship) which is an unforgivable sin. Nonetheless, the Prophet's words makes it clear the love and commitment a wife must have towards her husband. This is much easier for her to do if her husband is doing his part as being a loving father and husband in accordance with the saying of the Messenger of Allah (peace be upon him): "the best of you is that who is the kindest to his wife." Allah has made for you from yourselves mates and has made for you from your mates sons and grandchildren and has provided for you from the good things. Then in falsehood do they believe and in the favor of Allah they disbelieve? (16:72).

وَاللَّهُ جَعَلَ لَكُم مِّنْ أَنفُسِكُمْ أَزْوَاجًا وَجَعَلَ لَكُم مِّنْ أَزْوَاجِكُم بَنِينَ وَحَفَدَةً وَرَزَقَكُم مِّنَ الطَّيِّبَاتِ أَفَبِالْبَاطِلِ يُؤْمِنُونَ وَبِنِعْمَتِ اللَّهِ هُمْ يَكْفُرُونَ ﴿٧٢﴾

Lastly I ask Allah (swt) for forgiveness for any mistake I might have made, and pray that it will be acceptable to Him.

When the persecution of Qurayish intensified following the death of his uncle and his wife, the Prophet (peace be upon him) went to the tribe of At-Taif, hoping that would listen to him and support him. But they rejected him and told their children to throw rocks at him until blood flowed to his body and feet. The Prophet (peace be upon him) sought refuge in one of the gardens of At-Taif, and then he said the following beautiful and humble prayer to Allah:

اَللّٰهُمَّ اِلَيْكَ اَشْكُوْ ضَعْفَ قُوَّتِىْ وَقِلَّةَ حِيْلَتِىْ وَهَوَانِىْ عَلَى النَّاسِ يَاأَرْحَمَ الرَّاحِمِيْنَ أَنْتَ رَبُّ الْمُسْتَضْعَفِيْنَ وَأَنْتَ رَبِّىْ اِلَى مَنْ تَكِلُنِىْ اِلٰى بَعِيْدٍ يَتَجَهَّمُنِىْ أَمْ اِلَى عَدُوٍّ مَلَّكْتَهُ أَمْرِىْ اِنْ لَّمْ يَكُنْ بِكَ عَلَىَّ غَضَبٌ فَلَا أُبَالِىْ وَلٰكِنَّ عَافِيَتَكَ هِىَ أَوْسَعُ لِىْ أَعُوْذُ بِنُوْرِ وَجْهِكَ الَّذِىْ أَشْرَقَتْ لَهُ الظُّلُمَاتُ وَصَلَحَ عَلَيْهِ أَمْرُ الدُّنْيَا وَالْاٰخِرَةِ مِنْ أَنْ تُنْزِلَ بِىْ غَضَبَكَ أَوْ يَحِلَّ عَلَىَّ سَخَطَكَ لَكَ الْعُتْبٰى حَتّٰى تَرْضٰى وَلَا حَوْلَ وَلَا قُوَّةَ اِلَّا بِكَ

"O'Allah, to You do I complain of my weakness, little resource and lowliness before men. O'Most Merciful of those who show mercy, You are the Lord of the weak and You are my Lord. To whom will You leave me? To a far-off stranger who will mistreat me? Or to an enemy to whom You have granted power over me? If You are not angry with me, then I care not, but Your favour is better for me. I seek refuge in the Light of Your Countenance by which the darkness is illumined and the things of this world and the next are set aright, lest Your anger descend upon me, or Your wrath light upon me. It is You Whom we beseech until You are well pleased. There is no power, and no strength except in You."

Published for Allah (SWT), not for profit

www.ingramcontent.com/pod-product-compliance
Lightning Source LLC
Chambersburg PA
CBHW050801160426
43192CB00010B/1604